APPORTIONMENT
AND
REPRESENTATIVE
GOVERNMENT

By

Alfred de Grazia

FREDERICK A. PRAEGER, *Publisher*
New York

BOOKS THAT MATTER

Published in the United States of America in 1963 by
Frederick A. Praeger, Inc., Publisher
64 University Place, New York 3, N.Y.

© 1962, 1963 by Alfred de Grazia.

Library of Congress Catalog Card Number: 63-12709

Manufactured in the United States of America

FOREWORD

In concluding a history of ideas of representation in America, I once wrote that the idea of direct and equal representation "sufficed to correct many historical abuses against the individual and to direct a society in its communal, agricultural state." It "is still a powerful influence over the minds of many Americans." However, it "can be said to defeat itself when it makes exclusive claims over the whole field of representation, and when it attempts to deny new influences in areas where its own ineptitude is apparent and where a general negligence is encountered. . . . Our study of many ideas of representation shows that both the public and its leaders —political and intellectual—are prone to apply wholesale remedies. . . . Imitation, formalism, exaggeration, and conformity have ruled the history of representation. The only antidote is the flexible and imaginative prescription of the appropriate remedies in the particular context. The best method for determining the nature of such remedies is the collaboration of associated social scientists under political direction for the correction of a unique condition." [1]

Twelve years later I read with some astonishment of the Supreme Court's decision in the case of *Baker* v. *Carr*.[2] The highest Court, it appeared, had singled out for approval the doctrine of direct and equal representation as the basis of realigning the State legislatures. As if to celebrate the event, a flock of publications, conferences, and litigation rose up.

With few exceptions, the legal briefs and numerous research reports that I have since read have been deplorably shallow and unobjective. Our national history has been rummaged largely with an eye toward illustrating the feelings for numerical equality to be found among the people. But the case on apportionment is far from closed. What stands now cannot be permitted to represent all that political science has to say about apportionment and representative government. I felt this strongly while serving as consult-

---

[1] *Public and Republic* (New York, 1950), 252, 257, 258.
[2] 369 U.S. 186 (1962).

v

ant with the Office of the Attorney General of the State of New York on the apportionment provisions of the New York Constitution. The continuation of the present study was made possible by a grant from the American Enterprise Institute for Public Policy Research.

Thanks are owing to several advisers and assistants on this study. Irving Galt, Assistant Solicitor General of New York State, recognized earlier perhaps than any other legal officer of the country the need to employ new forms of evidence in apportionment cases. Sheldon Raab, Deputy Assistant Attorney General of New York State, gave sympathetic counsel at various stages of the work. Professor Joseph Tanenhaus of New York University read and criticized effectively the manuscript. Professor Charles S. Hyneman of Indiana University kindly provided an essential analysis, as did Professor Ralph Goldman of San Francisco State College. E. Blythe Stason, Dean Emeritus of the University of Michigan Law School assisted at several points. Dr. Felix Morley gave unstintingly of his great skills and experience as educator and publicist to the improvement of the final book. John S. Appel of the *American Behavioral Scientist* staff doubled his work over a period of time to afford me research assistance. I am also grateful to Julia Martinez and Victoria de Grazia for their assistance. Nor should I fail to thank the National Municipal League, so roundly criticized in this work, for making available to various scholars, including myself, a superior collection of court cases and other material. I still have hopes that the League will find new paths to its ultimate goals of better city government, with which I am strongly in sympathy.

I do not regard the present study as definitive. It is too close to the heat of controversy to observe all that is occurring. More important, the state of exact knowledge concerning apportionment is insufficient to guide public policy reliably. I can only hope that the book will serve in this present political emergency until more systematic, empirical, and elaborate studies will have appeared.

Alfred de Grazia

December 10, 1962

A Prefatory Note on *Baker v. Carr*

(369 U.S. 186, 1962)

This book is intended to examine the fundamentals of apportionment in relation to representative government. It is, however, permeated by the problems raised in the case of *Baker v. Carr.* Although those are taken up within the general organization of the book, it is well to have them in mind from the beginning.

The Tennessee Constitution provides for an apportionment of State Senate and House seats on the basis largely of equal-population districts and county boundaries. Reapportionment is constitutionally required every ten years (or so), and is to be performed by the legislature. The legislature did reapportion on several occasions between 1871 and 1901, but then ceased to do so until 1961, when certain voters brought suit before the U.S. District Court for the Middle District of Tennessee. They sought a declaratory judgment against State officials under the Fourteenth Amendment's guarantee against any State's denying to persons within its jurisdiction the equal protection of the laws. The lower court held that it lacked jurisdiction of the case and that no claim was stated upon which relief could be granted. The plaintiffs, Baker *et al.,* appealed the decision.

In *Baker v. Carr,* the Supreme Court held that the federal district court in Tennessee had jurisdiction. Voters had standing to bring the suit. And the case presented a justiciable question. The lower court's decision was reversed and the case remanded for further proceedings.

In the process of determining that jurisidiction was federal, the Court was impelled to assert its right to apply the Constitution to the organization of State legislatures. In the process of admitting the standing of the plaintiffs, it was impelled to find a possibility of denial of constitutional equality in systems of apportionment. In the process of affirming justiciability, it was impelled to deny pleas that apportionment systems were heavily political in nature and that intervention in them might prove too embarrassing and complex to suffer. In an extensive dissent, Justice Frankfurter denied the justiciability of this and similar cases.

Several closely related questions arose and were differently answered, among both the concurring Justices and the dissenting ones. Most important were the matter of the limits of Federal Court control over State legislative structures and the question of whether the doctrine of equal-population districts was to some degree required in apportionment by the equal-protection clause. Justices Clark and Harlan especially disputed the question whether the Tennessee apportionment then in effect was "rational" within the meaning of the Constitution. Opinions were also expressed, particularly by Justice Douglas, on the question whether invidious discrimination against the plaintiffs could be said to exist, insofar as various harmful effects could be said to be engendered by the apportionment system among persons in districts of larger than average population.

Thus to the question of what are the limits of federal judicial control over State governmental organization are attached the questions of what is apportionment, when is apportionment rational, what are its effects on society, and how should it be arranged.

Contents

List of Figures and Tables

1.

THE RUDIMENTS OF APPORTIONMENT

APPORTIONMENT FEVER STRUCK the State of Oregon last year. The Legislative Counsel Committee of the State, seeking to reduce to manageable proportions its task of assisting persons in the drafting of proposed apportionments, issued a "Legislative Reapportionment Do-It-Yourself Kit." Wrote the Committee, "Dear Do-It-Yourselfer . . . The Legislative Counsel Committee and its staff hope that this kit will answer some of your questions and afford some assistance to you in the event you wish to try your hand at formulating new apportionments."

The apportionment of legislatures is fascinating to the informed and uninformed alike. It is a task that appears simple, concrete, and logical—more a game than a task. But no sooner does one begin to play the game than he discovers how ramified its meanings, and disputed its rules. As the final discouragement, he sooner or later encounters a number of gentlemen who do not think it is funny at all and have political muscles to emphasize their seriousness—the legislators themselves.

Figure 1

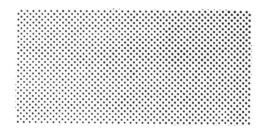

To demonstrate how apportionment begins, let us examine Figure 1. It consists of 1,565 dots more or less. Each dot stands for a person. All of them have a legislative assembly of five members. How can they be apportioned? Under the doctrine of absolute equal populations, to apportion this group, you should divide the population of 1,565 by the number of seats to be filled and then take any set of 313 people to make up each constituency, the only rule being "Don't count the same people in two constituencies." So a given constituency will be made up of 313 of the various types of persons found in the jurisdiction. The only thing they will have in common by contrast with the members of the other four constituencies is that they are charged with electing a legislator. This is superficially the most "in-human" apportionment possible. An enormous number of different apportionments could be made under its method.

2

Let us change the meaning of the dots. Let each dot stand for 5,000 people. That gives 7,825,000, almost exactly the population of Michigan in 1960, by a remarkable coincidence.

Thereupon we can apportion the legislature of the State of Michigan according to the absolute principle of equal populations. If the House of Representatives consists of 100 members, then we should place 78,250 people into each district. So we take a pencil, and beginning with any dot, circle that dot and 15 other dots to give the quota for a seat in the make-believe House of Representatives.

But who are these people; why are they in groups of 5,000; where do they live; how will they vote; what will the effect be? Never mind, this is a game of numbers, not politics; people are so many potatoes in a bushel. There are, by the way, trillions of possible combinations that fulfill the requirements as here stated.

Let us structure the problem a little more than the principle of equal populations deserves. Let us place people on a map of Michigan where they live, as in Figure 2. In it, each dot stands for 5,000 people again. Now again, the principle of equal populations says: draw any line anywhere, regardless of even the county lines you see on the map; just be sure you have only x dots. Again trillions of combinations are possible, none with any more meaning than any other, *unless additional rules are laid down.* The average intelligent person, given this task, will see the dilemma and immediately commences to set forth new rules. He says:

    1. Let's make a rule that the dots have to be as close together as possible. (A rule of *community, compactness, contiguity,* and *convenience.*)

    2. Let's make a rule that where other significant boundaries of going concerns exist, we should prefer to keep all the dots on one side instead of crossing back and forth. (A rule of *community* and *governmental efficiency.*)

    3. Let's make a rule that we shall not count in the dots any elements that move in and out of counties and State but only those that are people who have lived there for a year. (A *residence* rule.)

    4. We have to have a rule about what to do with fractions too, since, try as we may, some districts have more people than others. (A rule for *distributed fractions.*)

3

Figure 2

DISTRIBUTION OF POPULATION IN MICHIGAN BY COUNTIES: 1960

One dot represents 5,000 persons or major fraction thereof.

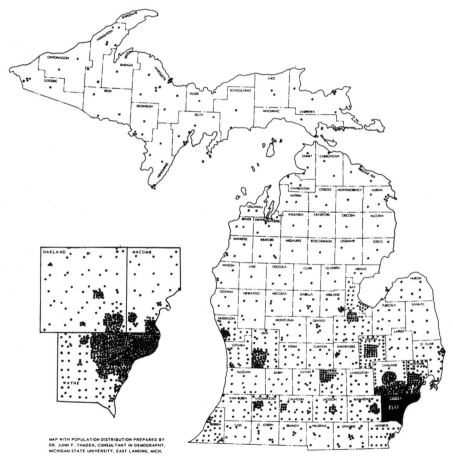

MAP WITH POPULATION DISTRIBUTION PREPARED BY
DR. JOHN F. THADEN, CONSULTANT IN DEMOGRAPHY,
MICHIGAN STATE UNIVERSITY, EAST LANSING, MICH.

Rules 5, 6, 7, 8, etc., etc., . . . As our average intelligent person moves into the problem, he becomes of much more than average intelligence. He sees that he has to make dozens of rules, and that, starting from his very first rule, he has been making public policy, not mere calculations. As the Special Master appointed in the Wisconsin case reported: "Redistricting is not a mere exercise in mathematics or logic, nor does it involve only the finding of facts." [1] One soon discovers, if he does not surmise as much from the beginning, that public policy is heavily involved and that many other people will not agree with his policies.

Actually the whole process depicted here could be performed more flamboyantly, using electronic computers. First, we should start with a list of all people in the State and perform 99 successive lotteries. These would be random constituencies of the State. (But note two big, debatable presumptions already. Why random? Why shouldn't steps be taken to avoid getting random groups, on grounds that we do not want each constituency to be like every other? Secondly, there would already have to be agreement on eliminating children and all others who are to be deprived of suffrage or who are non-voters.) The method would unite equal populations who would in each case mirror perfectly the population of the State. (Any random sample of 100,000 of a population of 9,000,000 would send a scientific sample survey expert into transports of joy.) Presumably, the equal-populations backers would want to add a customary rule—territorial residence. So the computer would exhibit its finer possibilities along the lines of the following simplified program.

Drawing of State apportionment boundaries by computer:
(Feasible for all jurisdictions, including the U.S.A.) [2]

Purpose: Place all People of State in Equal Population Districts as They Fall on the Geographical Map of the State.

---

[1] State of Wisconsin v. Zimmerman (U.S. Dist. Gt., Spec. Master Rept., Pt. II), paragraph 61.

[2] For those who wish not only to do their own apportionment but want to computerize the task, the following works, among others, may be recommended: Herbert D. Leeds and G. M. Weinberg, *Computer Programming*

A. Data (Input) to be stored in machine:
   Pinpointing of location on a grid of all persons in the State eligible to vote.

B. Instructions to machine:

   (1) Assign all persons with a given grid characteristic (a set of numbers) to one of x districts (x = No. of districts in the state).

   (2) Subtract individual A (defined as the last individual assigned to his district) from district X_1, reallocate him to district X_2 (defined as the district into which he would have fallen had he not been picked for X_1).

   (3) Recompute all the new district boundaries resulting from moving A from X_1 to X_2.

   (4) Repeat the last two procedures until you have all possible combinations (outputs). There are many millions of them, all conforming strictly to the original purpose of creating equal population districts based on territory.

C. Query: Which of these millions should be chosen? (See 7 below)

D. Additional purpose: To create a political situation favoring one party.

   (5) Assign each voter an R (Republican) or D (Democratic), designating his party (new input), with his number and instruct machine to eliminate all equal population apportionment combinations that do not concentrate the opposition party members into districts to the extent of 80 percent. Result (output): the opposition party members are massed into a few districts and the party to be favored will win consistently a majority of seats.

E. Alternative purpose (instead of D above): To group people around the already existing communities.

   (6) Assign a grid number to X "most important" centers of commerce and culture (new input). Instruct machine to

---

Fundamentals (New York, 1961); Robert Nathan and Elizabeth Hanes, *Computer Programming Handbook* (New York, 1962). For a detailed example of the construction of a computer model of voting behavior and its application, the interested technical reader should be sure to see pages 123-179 of W. N. McPhee and W. A. Glaser, eds., *Public Opinion and Congressional Elections* (New York, 1962).

assign people to their nearest community but not let anybody be farther than Y grid points from their center. Result (output): people are massed into districts around large centers. Districts are very uneven in population.

F. Which to be chosen?

(7) Reverting to 4, one way to choose the legal districting plan-to-be is by drawing one "winning plan" from the multitude. This could actually be done in advance by drawing one individual in the State by lot and making him or her the axis of the winning system. This would save much machine time.

Note that there would be many chances of unfavorable consequences under "B" above. Since this is applying the theory of equal territorial populations, that is all that is guaranteed. For the defenders of this belief, there is presumably no problem. For others there may be some distress owing to the possibility that the districts will not correspond to terrain differences, governmental groupings, ethnic differences, community or neighborhood groupings, economic similarities, political-historical traditions, and other characteristics that they believe should be reflected in apportionment. They may prefer plan "D" or "E" or any combination of these and other plans.

Is there then no use for the machines except to assist our theoretical thinking and to expose some logical absurdities? Yes, there may be. Following upon an initial period of research on computer possibilities in this area, it may be possible to set up some day a clear set of authoritative instructions for the machine that will electronically arrange the population into constituencies of certain traits. This "set of instructions" would be nothing other than what we shall call in the book *the policy of the constitutional authorities* regarding "how the government should be basically organized to do what,"[3] carried over from the whole theory of representative government to the sub-sub-field of apportionment.

Until a machine can do humane work, however, it is best to limit its use strictly and so also limit the use of machine-like theories that try to organize society. American society is not a collection of

---

[3] Cf. Alfred de Grazia, "Law and Behavior: A Unified Approach to Their Study," III *American Behavioral Scientist PROD*, May 1960, 3.

faceless particles. It is composed of highly diverse and yet inter-connected sets of people. A political theory suggesting that people are interchangeable like nuts and bolts is likely to be both fallacious and detrimental to the personal happiness of the citizenry.[4]

---

[4] Cf. Alfred de Grazia, "Mathematical Derivation of an Election System," *Isis,* June 1953, 42.

2.

REPRESENTATIVE DEMOCRACY AND APPORTIONMENT THEORY

THE SYSTEM CALLED DEMOCRATIC representative government is probably the most complicated political structure ever deliberately employed by man. An ICBM missile is simple by comparison: its arrangements of parts are tangible; cause and effects are more evident; human history does not play as large a part in its construction. It is quite necessary, therefore, to know something of the whole of representative government before attempting to examine one of its parts; apportionment cannot be understood without a larger comprehension of democratic representative government.

Politics in general is the quest for influence in government.[1] It embraces all behavior from the naked struggle for personal power to the rule-bound conduct of lawyers in a neutral court of law. We can say of politics, however, that its intent is always to discriminate; everybody involved in politics is under some necessity of seeking to preserve or change his position relative to the position of others; he must therefore act to help or to harm some interest, or else get out of politics. Good men, well-meaning men, and fanatics have often tried to destroy politics—thinking thereby to leave only the Truth, the true and one way—but they have inevitably failed or set up merely a new type of political system, screened by changes in words, where discrimination is still practiced on behalf of somebody and to the detriment of somebody else.

Representative government is an ordering of political relations. It is a system of devices and procedures (such as a legislature) intended to channel numerous opinions, interests, and abilities of a country into the making and executing of public policy. The opposite of representative government is a political order that claims all the reason, justification, and causes of its actions are beyond the scope and intelligence of all ordinary people. Nowadays the world is composed almost exclusively of representative governments; the few exceptions such as Saudi Arabia are not important enough to recall to mind the great changes of the past century. It was as late as 1822 when the leading nations of Europe declared at the Congress of Verona their resolve to crush all representative governments.

Yet, if the world of politics today is the world of representative government, it is still not a satisfactory world. Absolute governments exist that make the Congress of Verona governments appear pathetic, and they carry the forms of representative government.

---

[1] Many people are "in politics" for reasons other than influence, of course; they may merely enjoy the company of others so engaged. But the essential reason and theme of politics is influence. Lawyers may practice law to earn money but they are forced into a framework of institutions designed to test cases and make judgments.

The Soviet Union, the People's Republic of China, Spain, and other nations are obviously of a different order of politics than the majority of Western European countries and the United States. Let us call these latter older versions of representative government *democratic* and ask what are the principal elements in their make-up.

Democratic representative government includes:

1. A pervasive doctrine of the consent of the people as the basis of government.
2. Provision for entry of various kinds of opinions and interests into the political process and legislation.
3. Limits on the extent to which dissenting groups can be coerced.
4. A rule of law, applicable to the government as well as the people.

In the American system of government, the consent of the people is implied in the widespread respect accorded to the opinions of the common man, and in the several ways provided for the population to enter individual judgments of public policies. Methods of petitioning, voting, referenda, assembly, and other devices, are designed not only to assist major popular expressions, but are also intended for every minor opinion and interest. At the same time, there are widespread attitudes against going too far in repressing minority views; furthermore, a separation of powers and checks and balances are provided in the structure of government to prevent any single group from imposing its view on the totality without enlisting extraordinary support in opinion and action from previously uncommitted leaders. Also a stability of the law is usually maintained. There is a strong effort to justify rules, regulations, and decisions upon established precedents, and to make them only according to certain procedures designed to protect the persons involved in legal contests.[2]

---

[2] Cf. Gaetano Mosca, *The Ruling Class* (trans. 1939) on the principles of juridical defense; A. V. Dicey, *Introduction to the Study of the Law of the Constitution* (1926); "Post-War Thinking About the Rule of Law," *Michigan Law Review,* February 1961, 485-654. Alfred de Grazia, *Elements of Political Science* (1952), Chap. 9 (rev. ed., Colliers, 2 vols., 1962, II, chap. 2).

Four general traits then define American democratic representative government (three, if popular consent and the entry of more special opinions are conceived as shading into one another). But the machinery for working out these general design features is greatly differentiated. Hundreds of working principles (procedures) are involved. Each one of them acts to admit, foster, transform, or check some kind of opinion or behavior that is using the system.

To put it another way, practically every type of human desire has entered, been affected by, and influenced the system. And practically every kind of desire has been fabricated into a device or setting on the machinery of government to alter the inputs and outputs of opinions and behaviors.

It would be out of place here to explain the wide variety of human goals that have gone into the creation of the federal system and the division of tasks between State and local governments, of the political party system, of the system of judges and courts, of President, cabinet, and civil service, of the rights and powers of non-governmental but socially important institutions, and of the manner of conducting legislative business with its important committee system and provisions for leadership. It should be quite clear, nevertheless, that representative government of the American type rises and falls by every one of these, each consisting in turn of a great many variable procedures. All of these procedures and devices of representative government have some meaning and effect, though the difference between the most important and least important may be very large. And it must be added that there is no easy way to determine the effects of any single procedure upon the whole of representative government, even though they are all there for a purpose, that purpose being to advance somebody's idea of the good government and the good life.

Perhaps I may be allowed to be more specific on that great body of practices that is one of the major elements of representative government, namely *the election system.* Take or give a few, the formal and informal devices that go into the construction of an election system, or appear from time to time in an election system, are as listed below. These can be divided generally into three

12

sections: those having to do with the character of the officer who is to be chosen, those determining the character of the constituency, and those prescribing the procedure of selection. Despite numbering over 100 items, the list has categories that are insufficiently detailed to contain all the variations in the methods of selecting officials. One could not apply the list to an office and emerge with a perfect description of how it is filled. For instance, the exact experience required of candidates for office could not be stated without a great amount of relatively unimportant detail; hence only descriptions of general categories of experience were called for.[3] In other words, the list is already pitched upwards in generality from the level on which *every* individual variation would be regarded as potentially important; the list is not, despite its length, practical for any unique case.

**Check List for the Description of a Method
of Selecting or Electing Public Officers** [4]

Character of Officer
    Title of position
    General location of constituency
    Tenure of Office:
        Indefinite, months or years, or other
    Minimum age requirement
    Citizenship requirement
    Type of residence requirement
    Political party:
        Membership required
        Party nomination needed
        Primary election provided
    Education
        Literacy and how tested
        Formal education
        Information
        Ability

---

[3] Gathering data on this type of item presents many of the same problems as coding an open-ended question in social surveys.

[4] A more detailed list with definitions is available in mimeographed form for researchers in this area, by addressing the Department of Government at New York University.

Fees, nominal or substantial
Sex limitations
Real property ownership
    Income
    Rent
    Number of acres
Personal property required and amount
Tax payment, amount required
Religious qualification
Functional proficiency
    Military, legal, religious, other professional, trades
    Master, managerial, business entrepreneurial, or other
Experience
    Seniority, private functional, private functional representative or
        official, public office holding, military, legal
    Religious, other professional, trades, managerial, business
    Entrepreneurial, fraternal, or other
Number of offices of the same qualification filled at the same time
(*)Number of officers appointed or elected at the same time from other
    levels of government
Number of officers of the same grade in the same constituency
General functions of the officer
    Major or minor policy
    Major or minor administrative
    Judicial, including judicial policy
    Primarily honorary
    Primarily delegative

Character of Constituency

Size of constituency in population
Approximate size of constituency in travel time (for historical cases
    adjust time according to the age)
Manner in which constituency is grouped and derived
    Historical
    By survey (including specifications of compactness and contiguity)
    Existing independent jurisdiction
    Sociological definition
General functions of constituency during the tenure of the officer
    Occupational
    Solely electoral
    Public policy
    Public executive
    Public juridical

Provisions for the adjustment of constituency specifications
    Periodic
    Automatic
    Authoritatively adjusted
    Natural constituencies or other
Residence qualifications of constituents
Age qualification of constituents
Political qualifications of constituents
    Party member
    Office holder, public or private
    Banning of outlawed party members
    Banning of outlawed political activists
Sex limitations on constituency
Educational limits
Penal or mental disqualifications
Citizenship requirements
Real property requirements
Personal property requirements
Tax paying requirements
Religious requirements
Functional proficiency
Experience of constituents
Requirement of belonging to special groups such as military, legal, religious, or trade
Instructions: voluntary, compulsory, or forbidden.

Procedures of Selection

The type of ballot
    None
    Official
    Candidate-provided
    Party-provided
    . Voter-provided
    Printed, balls or other kinds
Mode of casting ballot
    Viva voce
    No formal vote
    Secret
    Public or other type of tally
Election place
    Specified or unspecified
    Central, unassembled
    Mail, or other unassembled

Assembled
Size of voting district
Counting votes
    One vote to one candidate
    Weighted preferences on ballot
    Weighted preferences in counting
    One vote for list or slate
Election formula
    Unspecified majority
    Majority of electorate
    Majority of voters
    Majority of specified quorum
    Unspecified plurality
    Plurality of electorate
    Plurality of voters
    Plurality of specified quorum
    Two-thirds majority, unspecified
    Other two-thirds majority type
    Unspecified unanimity
    Unanimity of voters or electorate
    Unanimity of specified quorum
    A portion of constituents for officer selected to the total constituents
    Unspecified beyond "election"
    Unspecified beyond "appointment"
Limits on Campaigning
    Limitation of expenditures
        Amounts
        Types
        Reporting
    Limitation of propaganda
        Amounts
        Types
        Reporting
    Limitation of agitation (meetings, assemblies, etc.)
        Amounts
        Type

Despite its length, the list is not inclusive of the individual elements in each category. For example, in regard to the item marked (*) at least 16 combinations for holding elections on different levels of government are possible. Each combination results in different turnout, issues, and even candidates. Thus, uniting a local

16

and presidential election usually brings out a bigger vote, and of course this helps somebody and harms somebody else. An experienced politician can even recount times when a given candidate is selected because he can ride through on a combined presidential level-local election test but would fail on a local-election test. Again, the size of the constituency varies greatly, from perhaps 20 to 180,000,000. Changes of size produce changes of many other kinds in the election process result. The only recorded intervention of George Washington in the Constitutional Convention of 1787 was a final plea for changing the Representative quota from 40,000 to 30,000, to extend the number of possible defenders of popular interests.[5] Note, too, how many ways of counting the winner there are, the majority principle being common, but many other principles such as plurality being used. As with the 26-letter alphabet that could provide us with millions of words, the basic elements of any election system can provide millions of possible effects.

All of the arrangements of representative government are operated by human beings, of course, men and women of a great many skills and different personalities and backgrounds. The structure affects them and they affect the structure. The legislators, administrators, lobbyists, judges, politicians, journalists, and citizenry work in and out of the machinery, bringing into it the tone and traits of the larger culture and taking out of it some habits and attitudes that come from the special experience of governing and politiking. Changing a formal procedure of representative government is not followed automatically by a measured response in accord with the change, but rather more often by a set of responses of a diversionary, subversive, adjusting, changing kind, so that often, the more things are changed, the more they remain the same.

To summarize thus far: politics is the process of influencing; representative government is a complex system for aiding some types of influencing and discouraging others; no single element in the system can be considered in isolation without bearing in mind all

---

[5] Madison in Farrand, ed., *Records of the Federal Convention of 1787* (1937), II, 644.

of the activity it affects or is affected by; elections are a sub-system of devices within representative government. In setting forth proposals for procedural change in a political process, the perennial risk is that important implications of the novel proposals may be disregarded, and unforeseen effects of a damaging character may be produced.

Apportionment Defined

Apportionment is part of the system of elections in a representative government. It is therefore included in the list just preceding, although, as we shall show, its depth and variety are greater than indicated there. In the most abstract and general sense, apportionment is the division of a jurisdiction into groupings (constituencies) some of whose members are enabled to participate in a designation of officers of the jurisdiction.

Each term in the definition has ramifications of significance. Expanding it, we get: "A division *(some authoritative agency must act)* of a jurisdiction *(the extent of legal control, though the population on which the apportionment is based is on occasion distinct from the jurisdiction—for example, the U. S. Constitution has an exogamous feature in that the Electors of a State are compelled to vote for either a President or a Vice President not a resident of their State)* into groupings *(of varying political or functional kind; size; degree of cohesion, from tightly organized to almost random membership; with different tasks, such as solely to vote, or to run the government—legislatures can also be constituencies; and differently qualified members—educated men, registered voters, etc.)*, some of whose members *(not everyone can vote, whatever the type of grouping)* are enabled *(they are not all interested, nor are they usually compelled to be interested)* to participate *(many other things happen in an election besides the voting itself to determine the successful candidate)* in a designation *(nomination, election, preference)* of officers of the jurisdiction *(usually members of an assembly but also executives, judges, and other electors)*."

More concretely and normally in the United States, apportionment is the division of a population into constituencies whose electors will vote for members of an assembly.[6] Although sometimes the population is calculated in terms of the number of actual voters, registered voters, or qualified electors in the districts created by apportionment, recent systems of apportionment commonly use the total population as the numerical basis of division. To be inclusive in our concept of apportionment, we may regard constituencies of the whole State or nation as single-district apportionments, and we may also consider informal, non-legal divisions of the electorate as apportionments. However, the central problems of apportionments arise from the determination of the constituencies of legislative assemblies.

Historical and Comparative Theory

Therefore, save in the case of a district of the whole State or nation, apportionment is invariably a recognition or solicitation of separatist groupings in a society. Some statesmen and writers, among them Rousseau, Gambetta, and a number of leading 18th century revolutionaries in America, England, and France, believed apportionment only a necessary evil. Forced to admit the demand and need for apportionment, they sometimes tried to cancel its effects. For instance, the French Constitution of 1793, after providing territorial apportionment, solemnly declared that the "representatives elected in the departments are not representatives of a particular department, but of the entire nation, and they must not be given any mandate." This miracle, however, did not appear. History could not have given hope of it then nor can it now. Apportionment in some form remains an absolute requirement of representative government. And apportionment is separatistic in design and effects, just as are other stages in the process of representation.

---

[6] The following several pages are based on Alfred de Grazia, "Theory of Apportionment," 17 *Law and Contemporary Problems* (1952), 256. Sometimes, as in New York State, a distinction is made between apportionment and districting, where the former allocates seats to a sub-jurisdiction such as a county, and the sub-jurisdiction further divides its population into specific constituencies. In our terms, this is a two-stage apportionment.

Apportionment exchanges another important feature with the process of representation. A criterion of apportionment always contains a value. Representation may be defined as a relationship between an official and a citizen in which the actions of the official accord with the desires of the citizen.[7] The relationship is a particular one, varying among individuals, and no device of representation extends to all persons equally. Every step in the process of granting representation to a citizen or group of citizens is a controversial one. From the determination of who shall vote to the provisions for control of the representative after he has been elected, the process of representation is subjected to a struggle over values, so that ultimately the system of representation favors in each detail some citizens over others, or extracts for favorable attention in policy-making certain attributes of individuals rather than other attributes. No system of apportionment and no system of suffrage, balloting, or counting is neutral. The process of apportionment, like the other stages in the process of representation, is a point of entry for preferred social values. Any existing system of apportionment, whether legal, illegal, or extra-legal, institutionalizes the values of some groups in the jurisdiction.

An examination of the criteria by which constituencies are divided may clarify the meaning of the foregoing remarks. The criteria underlying a system of apportionment consists of one or more of the following: territorial surveys; governmental boundaries; official bodies; functional divisions of the population; and free population alignments. Of these five criteria, territorial surveys are most common in modern times. "Artificial" areas are cut out of the map and their populations serve as constituencies. Historically this method of creating constituencies has been associated with the rise of egalitarian democracy.[8] The territorial survey is resorted to in order to divide the population into contiguous districts composed of equal numbers of voters. Since this criterion is so widely used and involves the most important current problems, its discussion may be postponed until the other criteria are described and analyzed.

---

[7] H. F. Gosnell, *Democracy: Threshold of Freedom* (1948), chaps. 7, 9, 11, and 12; A. de Grazia, *Public and Republic, op. cit.*, chap. 1.

[8] A. de Grazia, *Public and Republic, op. cit.*, 24, 26, 49, 106-108.

Apportionment by governmental boundaries is a part of all apportionment systems. The constituency of a nationally elective officer is the nation and the constituency of a local government executive is often the total electorate of his city or village. Thus the American governor is elected by the voters of his State as a whole; and an American mayor is often elected by the total electorate of the city. This constituency of the whole is important politically if only because the officer acquires a large increment of prestige and authority from expressing some of the desires and sentiments of the collectivity of voters. Theodore Roosevelt wrote that "the executive is or ought to be peculiarly representative of the people as a whole." [9]

Corporate or collegial bodies, such as the American State legislatures, also use the criterion of governmental boundaries in apportioning seats. A favored device of early American State governments was to apportion seats solely according to the county and town boundaries in one or both houses of the State legislature.[10] This procedure was abandoned in most State governments, on grounds that it invariably and openly worked to the disadvantage of governmental units of heavy population density. Yet it is well to note that in most cases where the major criterion of apportionment is the territorial survey, the law may require some attention to the boundaries of existing units of government in drawing district lines.[11]

In late medieval times, governmental boundaries were the favored criteria in the representative governments that were then developing. [12] In England corporate towns or boroughs that were so

[9] Theodore Roosevelt, *Autobiography* (1919), 306.

[10] Robert Luce, *Legislative Principles* (1930), chaps. 15-17.

[11] See Table I below.

[12] Cf. M. V. Clarke, *Medieval Representation and Consent* (1936); F. P. G. Guizot, *Histoire des origines du gouvernement representatif en Europe* (1851); May McKisack, *Parliamentary Representation of the English Boroughs During the Middle Ages* (1932); E. and A. G. Porritt, *The Unreformed House of Commons*, I (1903); C. A. Beard and J. D. Lewis, "Representative Government in Evolution," XVI *American Political Science Review* (1932), 223.

privileged by royal grant and the historic counties were each entitled to send two members to the House of Commons. Federal governments such as the United States are outstanding exemplifications of the use of governmental boundaries. Each State in the American union is authorized two United States Senators, and one seat in the House of Representatives regardless of size or population. Until the passage of the Seventeenth Amendment, the criterion of governmental boundaries was supplemented by the requirement of election by the State legislatures.

Election by the State legislature constituted a second criterion of apportionment which overlapped with the State-wide character of the office. It could be called apportionment in terms of official bodies. The apportionment of the American Senate was not unique in this respect, however. The electoral college that serves in law as the constituency of the President is another example of such an official body. However, whereas the State legislatures were standing bodies, the electoral college is an *ad hoc* agency, created specifically to elect the President. Both the permanent and *ad hoc* types are found as the electing agents elsewhere. The French system of indirect elections of the national Senate and Council of the Republic is founded upon electoral colleges composed of various officials and persons designated by local councils. The French system took much of its original inspiration from Condorcet, who was an admirer of the American system of electing the President.

The criterion used to create the apportionment is that the electors be previously designated to an agency charged with the elective function. When creating such special constituencies of a collegial body, the expectation is that the new constituencies will differ remarkably from their own constituencies, that they will be less rash, more discerning, and more knowledgeable. However, many more executive leaders or single officials are elected indirectly than are collegial bodies. The English prime minister, the European premiers, the *burgermeisters,* and some American mayors, and city managers are examples. The double apportionment of constituencies required of the indirect election of each member of a collegial body seems most often to be uneconomical and cumbersome, apart from its non-populist slant. Hence the *ad hoc* form is rarely used. More common is the use of a lower house to elect an upper house, or to create cabinets and councils, as exemplified so abundantly in the Russian hierarchy of soviets and presidia.

A fourth criterion by which constituencies may be cut out of a given population is by functional divisions. Functional groupings are non-territorial aggregates of persons who share social or economic interests. The degree of cohesion of the aggregates may vary widely, and different systems of apportionment of a functional kind make differing allowances for such varying cohesion. Thus, an ancient and persisting example of apportionment is by social estates. The early parliaments of the 13th century included, besides the commons, the estates of the nobility and clergy, sometimes organized separately and sometimes together. A fairly rigid class system stratified the population for purposes of apportionment. A much looser type of recognition of functional differences in apportionment is that which assigns representatives to localities on the basis of the amount of taxes the locality pays. For example, under the French Constitution of 1793 each department was allotted a basic minimum of representatives in the National Assembly, then allotted additional seats according to its population, and finally allotted seats according to the total taxes it paid. This last provision of the Constitution benefited the wealthier regions, and presumably indirectly the wealthier classes. In South Carolina from 1808 until the Civil War, a system quite similar prevailed in the apportionment for the lower house. One-half the total delegates were assigned to the districts and parishes in proportion to the whole population and the other half in proportion to the average of taxes paid for the ten years preceding the decennial reapportionments.[13] The pre-World War I Prussian system of apportionment assigned representation on the basis of taxation also. The largest taxpayers, paying one-third of

---

[13] C. S. Boucher, *Sectionalism, Representation, and the Electoral Question in Ante-Bellum South Carolina,* IV Washington University Studies II (1916).

the total taxes, obtained the right to elect one-third of the delegates to the *Landtag,* the middle tax-paying group another third, and the lowest another third. The top group consisted of about 6 percent of the total electorate. In the American Constitutional Convention of 1787, consideration was given to the possibility of allocating representation according to the taxes paid by a State, but, partly because tax-paying areas were believed to coincide with areas of high population density, population was chosen as the basis for representation.[14] Today New Hampshire bases the apportionment of its Senate on 24 districts paying equal sums of direct taxes.[15]

Many other forms of apportionment based on functional groups have been employed. Not only estate and tax-paying groups but also nationality groups, university groups, professional groups, factory groups, and general occupational groups have been used as the criteria. Thus in Moravia, after World War I, the Germans and Czechs were given each a number of seats and cross-nationality voting was forbidden, and Turks and Jews were represented specially in the Greek Parliament. In Cyprus today, Greeks and Turks form distinct constituencies. The English universities used to be represented by their own districts, as did William and Mary College once in the United States. Professional groups have sent representatives to the Greek, Hungarian, and Italian legislatures at one time and the practice continues in Ireland and Portugal. Russian factories until 1936 sent delegates to the local soviets or councils, that in turn elected the delegates to higher councils. Under the Fascist regime in Italy, the Chamber of Corporations was a national legislature based on constituencies composed of major occupations. This was the most complete attempt to this date to practice functional apportionment exclusive of territorial influences. In America the various authorities acting under the National Industrial Re-

---

[14] II *Records of the Federal Convention of 1787,* 582, 587.

[15] N. H. Constitution, Pt. II, art. 26. The provision was contested and upheld by the N. H. Supreme Court in Levitt v. Maynard (July 16, 1962). In this case as in a number of others, I am indebted for the text of the decision to a set of three mimeographed volumes of Court Decisions on Legislative Apportionment published by the *National Municipal League.*

covery Administration from 1933 to 1935 gave certain powers over prices, wage and work standards, and fair trade practices to groups composed of the delegates of the various firms of different industries. Variations of this practice have continued to this day in many jurisdictions.[16]

A final criterion of apportionment is free population alignments. Advocates of this criterion deem it unjust to force constituencies out of social criteria such as geography or social estate or property. Rather, individuals ought themselves to choose their constituency according to whatever their dominant motive may be at the time of casting their ballot. This criterion is basic to systems of proportional representation, wherein the free and personal apportionment is joined with a multi-member district and a preferential vote to permit the representation of any group that achieves a quota of votes roughly equivalent to the total district vote divided by the number of seats to be filled. The criterion cannot be employed in majority elections. Election of several representatives at large, in which the constituency for a legislature is a single electorate in its entirety, produces generally a monopoly representation of the major political grouping of the geographical constituency. Hence it resembles territorial apportionment.

The anti-territorial characteristics of free apportionment have not been sufficiently realized. J. Francis Fisher, an early American inventor of a system of proportional representation, declared that "it is not land, nor the owners of it, who form our constituencies, but the citizens generally; and that the opinions, principles, and interests of the people, which really ought to find expression in their representatives, can never be expected to conform to any possible territorial division."[17] But in fact neither the free apportionment of

---

[16] Cf. J. A. C. Grant, "The Gild Returns to America," IV *Journal of Politics* (1942), 303; Arthur N. Holcombe, *Government in a Planned Democracy* (1934); A. de Grazia, *Public and Republic, op. cit.,* chap 8; Mary P. Follett, *The New State* (1918); Avery Leiserson, *Interest Representation in Administrative Regulation* (1942); and Louis Jaffe, "Law Making by Private Groups," LI *Harvard Law Review* (1937), 201.

[17] *The Degradation of Our Representative System and Its Reform* (1863), 48.

proportional representation, nor any other system of apportionment has been able, in law or in practice, to dissolve the territorial basis for apportionment. A closer scrutiny of territorial apportionment may reveal the foundations of its strength.

Apportionment by territorial survey, it was noted earlier, has replaced governmental boundaries as the prevailing criterion of apportionment. The survey method historically increased in use as individualism increased. The English Levellers of the mid-17th century were, to my knowledge, the first to demand a mathematical subdivision of the nation into election districts of equal population. The merchant and commercial classes did help to break the monopoly over representative government exercised from the 13th to the 18th centuries by the landed nobility and the untitled landlords, but they did not "rationalize" the representative system by reducing it to a numbers formula. The egalitarian democrats as typified by the Levellers did. The egalitarian democrats, with many supports of middle class origin to be sure, espoused a theory of representation that culminated in the individualism of the advocates of proportional representation such as Fisher and John Stuart Mill.

But the egalitarian democrats never went so far as their intellectual leaders, for their interest base was in agrarianism. Thomas Jefferson, it must be remembered, was a physiocrat, an agrarian, and then an advocate of individual representation based on the territorial survey. Territorial representation, with equal representation to all men, was the ideal formula for a democratic rural society and was espoused as such by early 19th century democrats in America and elsewhere. "Equal representation," wrote Jefferson to King on November 19, 1819, "is so fundamental a principle in a true republic that no prejudices can justify its violation because the prejudices themselves cannot be justified." [18] We cannot now know whether Jefferson's equally vehement agrarianism and dislike of cities would have changed his mind, when faced with the necessity either of carrying out the principle of equal representation and weakening

---

[18] Archives of the Huntington Library, San Marino, California; quoted by Robert de Vore, "Gallery Glimpses," *Washington Post.* April 4, 1943, 48.

the agrarian interest or else maintaining the preponderance of the agrarian element and violating his theory of representation.

Apart from its ultimate unagrarian operation when the cities had grown, apportionment by territorial survey, arising as it did out of the demands for individual equality, did some damage to localism. To maximize local influences and community spirit, apportionment should be based on local units of government, as was originally the case in a number of American States and is presently the case in several. Then all the electorate of a given locale, who are possessed already of a degree of solidarity from economic, social, and political causes, will project that solidarity into the national or State legislature and reinforce it thereby. Since many "natural" units of local governments are divided or combined in the geometry of apportionment, the full impact of localism on State or national legislatures is less than it might otherwise be. Nevertheless, territorial surveys that produce, in the language of the Congressional Apportionment Act of 1842 and other enactments, a "contiguous and compact territory containing as nearly as practicable an equal number of inhabitants." [19] will provide a considerable reflection of local interests.

The act of apportionment, to summarize the preceding discussion, consists of the postulation of certain basic values as deserving of disproportionate influence in the scheme of representative government, and of carrying them into effect in the division of constituencies. The several criteria and sub-criteria that may be used in any system of apportionment aim at long-range determination of the policy product of the government. Conflicting social groups and individual philosophies work constantly to preserve or change the established basis of apportionment. Basic changes in criteria of apportionment are part of the great historical revolutions. No act of apportionment, legal or illegal, is neutral with respect to all men.

This fact is clear even if apportionment is taken to include only the formal or legal apportioning decisions taken by agencies of the State, such as the legislature. The fact is more meaningful if one considers the unofficial apportioning that constantly occurs in a

---

[19] 5 Stat. 491 (1842).

society. Whatever the legal system of apportionment, other criteria will enter the system and modify it. For example, a legislature based solely on territorial apportionment will represent something of a sense of community. Although there may be some truth in the allegation that legislatures are separatistic by nature, it is nevertheless true in some respects that individual legislators are part of the total society; they have enduring connections with it, and are thus impelled by such internal compulsions as well as by the external forces contained in the pressures from their constituencies and other constituencies and persons to act in terms of some State-wide or national consensus. Similarly, although a territorial survey may be made without regard to any principle save territorial contiguity and equality of population, other interests will make themselves felt. The most conspicuous example of such interests in American experience is the pressure group and its lobby. The lobby, practically viewed, is based on a functional constituency, self-apportioned; the numerous lobbies of a complex society are usually representative of groups denied the status of legal constituencies.[20].

Also, the political process, reacting to the legal system of apportionment, sub-apportions the people of a society. For example, the technique of a balanced ticket, so common in American politics, overcomes the local territorial effects of the apportionment by survey by recognizing functional groupings in the society and apportioning candidates among them. Thus, within a given territorial district, a balanced ticket may include, as candidates for the various offices to be filled, persons from certain occupational groups, religions, income levels, nationalities, and right or left wing minorities. As it has developed historically, the territorial survey type of apportionment has granted emphasis to community representation and especially to local real property interests, but it has also been a loose kind of apportionment by contrast to other types and has permitted other criteria to be developed within its confines.

The unofficial apportionment that occurs within the legal system of apportionment is not the only change any legal system may be

---

[20] E. Pendleton Herring, *Group Representation Before Congress* (1929), 47, 50.

expected to undergo. Habituating themselves to the requirements of the law, various interests may work into the territorial system itself and derive benefit therefrom. A prominent historical example is the entrance of the commercial classes in England into the territorial apportionment system through the purchase of land.[21] By the time the rotten boroughs of England were eliminated in the 19th century, the major commercial interests were fairly well spoken for from seats in the Commons that they had previously acquired by purchase. And the House of Lords was composed in part of men who had risen in commerce and industry and had been granted titles for one reason or another. The present interests of the urban centers of the American States, as we shall see, sometimes venture for representation outside of their legal constituencies.

To suggest another case in which one type of apportionment may be transformed into another type by external forces, one may point to the careers of various kinds of proportional representation. Whereas the 19th century inventors of proportional representation viewed their work as fostering individualism and freedom of action in representative government, a major consequence of proportional representation has been the increase in cohesiveness of political groupings. Every effort is exerted to organize and discipline a quota of voters, because only a part of the voters, a quota, is needed to elect any single member; a plurality is not necessary. The Europeans, with their list systems of proportional representation, have gone further, and radically reduced non-partisanship elections.[22] They have sometimes permitted only party lists to be offered the voter. All votes for a party list are divided up by the quota, and the seats thereby won are given to the party's preferred candidates. This system is too far removed from the PR systems advocated in America to be fully employed in evaluating them.

---

[21] I. W. E. H. Lecky, *A History of England in the Eighteenth Century* (1888), 250.

[22] F. A. Hermens, *Democracy or Anarchy? A Study of Proportional Representation* (1941). Compare the defense of proportional representation by G. H. Hallett, "Is Proportional Representation a Trojan Horse?" VI *Social Research* (1939), 415. Also see M. Duverger, *Political Parties* (New York, 1954).

Finally, it must be realized that, since apportionment is only one stage of the process of representation, values that are blocked from entering politics on that level may seek and find other levels at which they may enter and be counted. To illustrate what is meant by this point, we may depict the various levels of the process of representation at which the substitution of a value denied elsewhere may occur. A group of small businessmen, engaged in commerce and trade, will not seek the same system as a group of farmers or workers. If their thinking were without internal conflict or ideological overtones, they would tend over a period of time to favor a system of apportionment, which, while in part based on territorial survey, would provide some disproportionate influence to those who pay more than average taxes. An arrangement such as that contained in the French Constitution of 1793 or the pre-World War Prussian system might be satisfactory. But if this were denied them, they could seek other means of influencing the structure of the representative system. They might seek property, tax, residence, or educational restrictions on the franchise. They might fight vigorously against limiting the franchise to landholders. They might agitate also against limiting legislative candidacies to possessors of land, but might favor limiting candidacies to property-holders. They might seek to place all major financial officers of the government upon the ballot, rather than limiting the election to top political officers alone. They might not favor strongly the secret ballot, since secrecy would deny them the opportunity to form opinions about the votes of those economically dependent upon them. They might well be puzzled by the kind of election system to prefer, since the workings of the majority system depend so much on the character of the franchise and the party system. Under a severely limited franchise, they might well prefer a majority or plurality system of election, as did the American merchants of the Revolutionary Period.

On the other hand, they would be generally unfavorable to any system that could allow more numerous groups than they to possess mandated or instructed representatives, whether such a system be of the plurality type or of proportional representation. They might well favor any or all of the numerous devices to limit the election

30

system to certain kinds of decisions. Thus they might prefer financial referenda if experience demonstrated such referenda to be free of mass controls. They might also favor bicameralism, uninstructed representatives, checking organs of government such as an appointed judiciary, or other devices to mitigate the effects of a universal suffrage. In short, every step of the process of representation would present arrangements that might or might not be specially adopted to their advantage. Other social interests, such as a group of coal miners or a learned profession, might behave similarly. History, to be sure, rarely shows cases of such complete addiction of any specific group to the total process of representation, but numerous groups have behaved analogously to the hypothetical case with respect to several stages.[23] And at any given point in time, when one examines the struggle centered about any particular feature of representative government, he finds a welter of interests engaged in determining the shape an existing or proposed channel of influence is to assume. It is in this sense that apportionment must take its place alongside numerous other variables that all together determine the long-range policy output of the government.

---

[23] J. Hogan, *Elections and Rrepresentation* (1945); Karl Braunias, *Das Parliamentarische Wahlrecht* (1932); Porritt and Porritt, *op. cit.;* Kirk H. Porter, *A History of Suffrage in the United States* (1918); Luce, *op. cit.*

3.

DOCTRINES AND IDEOLOGIES

EACH DEVICE IN APPORTIONMENT, as each in representative government, stands for a preference or an accord of preferences. Are these preferences disconnected or are they part of some larger system of beliefs? The answer is that they tend to be a part of larger belief-systems, even when their advocates do not realize it.

A *doctrine* is a belief that something *should* be; it is phrased in the language of political movements. Thus, "The State has to care for its citizens!" An ideology is a way of looking at the world through the glasses of one's wishes and doctrines.[1] It is an ensemble of psychologically related doctrines. A person may believe, for example that "A State that doesn't care for its citizens soon collapses" and that "The mass of people is rarely wrong." These and other beliefs, whether or not factually correct, make up a kind of democratic ideology. Far from being objectionable, a set of different but mutually supporting ideologies may be the firmest foundation for a way of government such as our own.[2]

The ideas of representation and apportionment that circulate today are without exception of ancient vintage. Actually, the belief in districts of equal population for election of legislators is a relative newcomer, being about 300 years old. It is part of the general complex of ideas about representative government that may be called egalitarian-majoritarian. As such, it stands in contrast with another popular doctrine and ideology, the traditional-organic, and yet another, the free-group belief. These clusters of ideas are not airtight. Still, many persons are likely to maintain psychologically and logically *related* ideas on the subject of representation. It is not likely, for example, that a man who believes in the principle of equal-populations districts will also believe in the freedom of the representative from the mandate of his constituency, or in the restriction of the suffrage. And it is unusual for him to assert the authority of non-elected courts to make public policy, and perhaps owing only to a momentary expediency, as in the present instance.[3]

Democratic Belief-Systems

That which I call the traditional-organic doctrine in representation and apportionment tends to prefer the established to the new. It emphasizes the complicated nature of representative systems and

---

[1] Cf. Karl Mannheim, *Ideology and Utopia* (1936); Ernst Cassirer, *Philosophy of the Enlightenment* (1951); Sebastian de Grazia, *The Political Community* (1948); Hans Vaihinger, *Philosophy of "As If"* (New York 1924).

[2] Alfred de Grazia, *Politics and Government*, Vol. I, Ch. 9.

[3] It must be fairly obvious that a large number of those presently applauding the courts for their "liberal" position must have attacked them in the thirties for blocking social legislation. Charles S. Hyneman analyzes this phenomenon in a forthcoming work, *The Supreme Court on Trial*.

the many fine and hardly recognized adjustments to the existing order of things that each part of the system has made over time. It tends therefore to be prejudiced against change and, in its most rigid form, to reject even the most careful and calculated plan of reform. Inasmuch as the sense of land and community is an ancient feeling, the traditional-organic mind is favorable to the weighting of these elements in representative systems. It is not impressed by schemes that do not recognize the importance of older community forms—the county, the State, the city as an organized organic settlement.

It is likely, therefore, that many of the defenders of the *status quo* in apportionment in the United States will come from the community-minded group, for the present systems of apportionment in America are historical and venerable, certainly, and lay stress upon a number of established community boundary lines. The New England town districts of Vermont, Rhode Island, and Connecticut would attract him. In fact, the first organic theorists of America were the early Puritans, with their doctrines of community, church-state union, and magistracy.[4]

At the same time, a consistent defender of the traditional-organic position must find much that is wrong in the present-day general set-up. He would not appreciate the ways in which district lines sometimes criss-cross the communities that to his way of thought are the natural constituencies of the county. Nor would he like certain other features of the representative system, apart from apportionment.

Defenders of the *status quo* would also include the free-group believers, although they too have their own reasons for being dissatisfied with the apportionment system. They would regret the lack of true community foundations in many existing apportionments, for example. They would also be concerned that the whole idea of group activity—which is what moves much of American politics—still is not approved by the country as an openly-held principle of

---

[4] Cf. V. Parrington, *The Colonial Mind* (1927); Perry Miller, *The New England Mind* (1939).

good government. They would assert with James Madison that society is ever-changing *and* always organized into more or less well-structured groups.[5] These associations, unions, corporations, churches, parties, and factions are the most important factors in the political process, and the representative system should be viewed as a process of accommodating them through institutional arrangements. These men would differ among themselves regarding the degree of group autonomy as such that they would permit; they would differ when assigning formal authority to the group, some feeling that the groups ought to be given formal authority and accountability in association with the government, others believing that they should enter the government only as unofficial and regulated pressures. They would be inclined to favor an apportionment system that would recognize differences of responsibility in society and provide for some weight to be given group leaders, the more active citizens, and to groups as electing bodies, that is, the constituencies. (The example given above, p. 31, would belong to this free-group view.)

The point of view that will occupy us most in this study is the egalitarian-majoritarian. It is providing the leading doctrines and slogans for the present offensive on apportionment that is agitating political and judicial leaders around the nation. Examples of its slogans are "One man—one vote"; "equal representation"; "voting equality"; "equal apportionment"; and so forth.

Typical of the form of thought is the following, the beginning passage in one of the hundred booklets of similar views on apportionment published around the country:

> Democratic theory rests on the assumption that the people are sovereign. From this fundamental tenet arise two corollary postulates of democracy. The first is that each person in the commonwealth is to count for one, and no more than one. This is the principle of numerical equality. The second is that decisions are reached by counting each person as one to determine which policies are sanctioned by the greater number of people. This is the

---

[5] See Footnote 16, p. 25. Cf. David Truman, *The Governmental Process* (1951); Alfred de Grazia, "Nature and Prospects of Political Interest Groups," 319 *Annals of the American Academy* (1958), 113; A. F. Bentley, *The Process of Government* (1908).

principle of majority rule. . . . When a man from district "A" represents 200,000 people and another from district "B" serves 400,000 people the democratic principle of numerical equality is subverted.[6]

The egalitarian-majoritarian view is that the machinery of representative government should be completely in the hands of and responsive to a majority of all the people. (This, we must remember, is in the realm of sheer doctrine.) In its fullest doctrinal form, it demands that all governing powers be placed in the hands of officers directly and frequently elected by the majority principle by the universal suffrage of population.

Today we are too far from the radical, socialist,[7] and populist movements of the 18th and 19th centuries to comprehend readily the complete and far-reaching ideology permeating them. We no longer hear widespread calls for a multiple executive, annual elections, an elective judiciary, the conversion of all important executive offices from appointment to election, the instruction of representatives on how to vote, the general use of the initiative and referendum, and the recall of public officers by popular petition and vote. Also, of course, some of the egalitarian beliefs have become standard practice—universal suffrage, direct election of U. S. Senators, and many constituencies composed of equal populations. The last, equal-population districts, have not been fully achieved, for many reasons that will be dealt with shortly. But, without doubt, the essential origins and arguments of the equal-populations doctrine presently being stressed in public affairs are part of the doctrines of the egalitarian-majoritarian movements of the past couple of centuries.

It must be admitted that, of the several views of apportionment described, the egalitarian is the most doctrinaire. Voiced originally and continuously on behalf of, if not by, "all the people," it possesses

---

[6] James W. Drury and James E. Titus, *Legislative Apportionment in Kansas: 1960,* Government Research Center, University of Kansas (Lawrence, Kansas, 1960), 9-10.

[7] Cf. for example, Karl Marx and F. Engels on the Paris Commune of 1870, where the Socialist tendency to espouse the ideas under discussion is to be seen.

36

an absolute quality not found in other viewpoints. Owing to its acceptance by many teachers and to its own nature, it pretends to a monopoly over the history of American thought. This it does despite a limited sense of reality and the most visionary proposals to be found in any of the views.[8]

Nevertheless, the essence of any ideology is its unconscious and tenacious grip on views both impractical and unreflective of the world of real events. Therefore, while we should say that all devices of apportionment are expressions of preference, and that an ideology contributes and organizes a group of preferences, we have to make also three further points: few people have pure ideologies; many people support particular devices with regard to only short-term effects; and devices of a certain kind may be preferred often because they simply are at hand, or as relatively inconsequential ingredients in a system already strongly pitched a contrary way.

Rationality

The term *"rational"* enters the discussion of apportionment particularly in connection with judicial appraisals of the constitutionality of a given system. The word *"rational"* is, of course, not a stranger to litigation, being one of those adjectives of expansible or collapsible nature necessary to judicial searching.[9]

When a court defines rationality, as we shall show below, it may be acting in an authoritative capacity whereupon we must say that as a legal matter rationality is whatever courts say it is in the instant case and whatever they may say it is in the next case.

However, there is some point to discussing rationality in apportionment as a logical, psychological, and empirical problem. When applied to the field of apportionment, the term might have several

---

[8] Robert G. McCloskey, "The Reapportionment Case," *Harvard Law Review*, November 1962, 71. "It is certainly untrue that 'one man, one vote' was regarded by the framers as an imperative basic principle for carrying on the day-to-day, year-to-year process of government; and it is at least dubious that any such principle became embodied in our constitutional tradition in the years that followed."

[9] Vaihinger, *op cit.*

meanings. None is absolutely right, and, unfortunately, none is absolutely clear. What we do learn is that by any token of rationality, except the defiance of all common and specialized meanings, nearly every system of apportionment is rational. The qualification "nearly" is only to give safety in those cases where evidence is lacking or the system is unstudied; there are, after all, many thousands of apportionment systems.

A first meaning is rational in an external philosophical sense: a *rational* action is one that finds a true and objective solution to some human problem, as when it is said that "a rational man prefers peace to war." Actually, what is meant is that a man who subscribes to our *reasons* for preferring peace to war is defined as rational. We know of no major philosophy that finds some particular device of representation, except possibly the basic principles of representative government itself, rational or irrational in this sense.

A second meaning of rational is traditional. An action or a formula for action may be said to be *rational* when it is accepted and recognized as the traditional way of performing a given set of operations. In the words of Edmund Burke, who insisted upon this type of rationality as often superior to other forms of rationality, and whose views have found a considerable element of support in American political and judicial doctrine over many years:

> . . . a nation is not an idea only of local extent, and individual momentary aggregation; but it is an idea of continuity, which extends in time as well as in numbers and in space. And this is a choice not of one day, or one set of people, not a tumultuary and giddy choice; it is a deliberate election of ages and generations; it is a constitution made by what is ten thousand times better than choice, it is made by the peculiar circumstances, occasions, tempers, dispositions, and moral, civic, and social habitudes of the people, which disclose themselves only in a long space of time. It is a vestment which accommodates itself to the body.[10]

Certainly the constitutional authorities of many jurisdictions have supported this form of rationality in their employment of apportionment formulas in the beginning and through the years. There was

---

[10] "On The Reform Of Representation In The House Of Commons," *Works,* Vol. VI, 146-47.

nothing new, unknown, untried, and unexpected about community formulas when adopted over the past couple of hundred years. They have been known, tried, and practiced in Europe, England, and America for centuries prior to their reformulation and adoption in the American and State Constitutions.

A third type of rationality recognizable in the literature of politics is individualistic rationality. A product of the French and American Enlightenment Period of the 18th century, it has carried down to the present time with great strength. Jeremy Bentham is a model of such thought. According to this type of rationality, an action or plan is rational when it is directed at producing direct gain to an individual in his own, subjective terms. The best social policy multiplies this individual effect to produce the greatest good of the greatest number. According to its terms, tradition is not to be considered but rather whether the mass of people is being served. How can this question ever be answered? Usually by voting and majority rule.

A fourth type of rationality is pragmatic and realistic. Here rationality means judging a system by its effects. Whatever works well is judged good. Who is to say whether a thing works well? Presumably the same people who passed on the individualistic benefits of an action above; that is, a majority or a ruling opinion group. The important difference is that these realistic rationalists are impatient with theory. They try to get along with a minimum of testing: "if the shoe fits, wear it; if it pinches, get another."

Still a fifth kind of rationality is statistical and sociological. If a goal is stated and a plan is accurately set up to achieve that goal, then the behavior is rational. This is called instrumentally rational. In demonstrating the rationality of an apportionment, we should have to establish only that the constitutional authorities had purposes in mind and used a certain formula of apportionment, in concert with a great many other devices, to bring about the fulfillment of these goals. Actually this seems to be the type of rationality that certain members of the Supreme Court of the United States in the case of *Baker* v. *Carr* had in mind. Let us try to paraphrase it: if a device of government is aimed, even if not with perfect clarity and knowledge, at producing certain effects in ways that are understandable, even if not perfectly scientific, that device is rational and all further devolutions of the device are rational within the same bounds. This instrumental *rationality* is the view adopted in this study.

Perhaps the problem of determining rationality may be clarified by resorting to the dispute over the rationality of the Constitution of the State of New York in respect to apportionment.[11] In 1894 a Constitutional Convention adopted and the people of the State approved a system that gave some governmental units more seats than a doctrine of equal-population districts would allow, and gave New York City less possibilities of earning new seats by population growth than were given to middle-sized cities.[12] In this plan, we see several types of motives that are clear enough to be listed, and we may even recognize in the formula of apportionment adopted in 1894 an expression of each of these motives translated into weighted quantities.

1. The first is the motive of permitting popular movements of opinions, beliefs, and desires to express themselves, and not only to express themselves, but, if intense and determined, to rule the State. Figure 3 shows that this motive was the most heavily discussed of all in the New York Constitutional Convention of 1894.

If more proof is needed, we should seek specifications regarding any later cases of intense and widespread public opinion that did

---

[11] Cf. *WMCA* v. *Simon,* 61 Civ. 1559, U.S. District Court, Southern District of New York.

[12] This' history and statistics of New York's apportionment have been studied with enormous patience and competence, though unfortunately from an exclusively egalitarian point of view, by Professor Ruth Silva, and are contained in an unpublished manuscript, in briefs of the plaintiffs in WMCA v. Simon (U.S. District Court, NY, July 1962), and in several articles in the *American Political Science Review* (1961) and *Fordham Law Review* (1962). The opinions of the three justices of the Federal District Court in the two WMCA v. Simon cases recast the salient history and statistics. The briefs entered by the State of New York per Mr. Irving Galt, Assistant Solicitor General, are along the line of argument ultimately presented by the court.

not reach sharply and successfully into the centers of governments. They are rare and unknown to this writer. The existing apportionment accords two-fifths of the legislative seats in the two houses of the legislature to the metropolis of New York. A union of heavy public sentiment in the City, if not blocked by its own representatives, can, when joined by a modest force elsewhere in the State, carry the day.

More directly again, resort to the language of the Constitutional Conventions of the last century reveals attention to public opinion and a desire to keep the flood-gates of opinion open enough to handle the greatest tides, though still keeping them within bounds.

2. At the same time, we see a local community motive in the apportionment formula. (See Figure 3, which shows it also was heavily discussed in the Convention.) We have stated earlier that this is a heritage of the Middle Ages. If the ancient Greeks and Romans had perfected some mode of achieving autonomous localities within the representative structure of a larger empire or republic, mankind might have been saved many centuries of disorder. The representation of communities was one of the greatest inventions of the late Middle Ages and has come down to the United States via the English parliamentary system of borough and shire representation and the American colonial and State system of representation of communities in government. Whether boroughs and towns or counties, the basic fact in all such situations is that an operative human system of communication, work, and thought is reflected in a larger network.

Whether the size of a unit should be small or large is not at issue here. Whatever the size, it can scarcely be doubted that the representation of the whole, rather than the part or nothing at all, of a community is effectively rational. Nor does the need of the local unit diminish because some other unit has grown to great size. We have gone a long way towards making atoms out of individuals in modern society; it is of little help in resisting this process to say that the benefit to be derived from atomizing more people is giving more power to individuals with the same problem in larger aggregates.

Figure 3

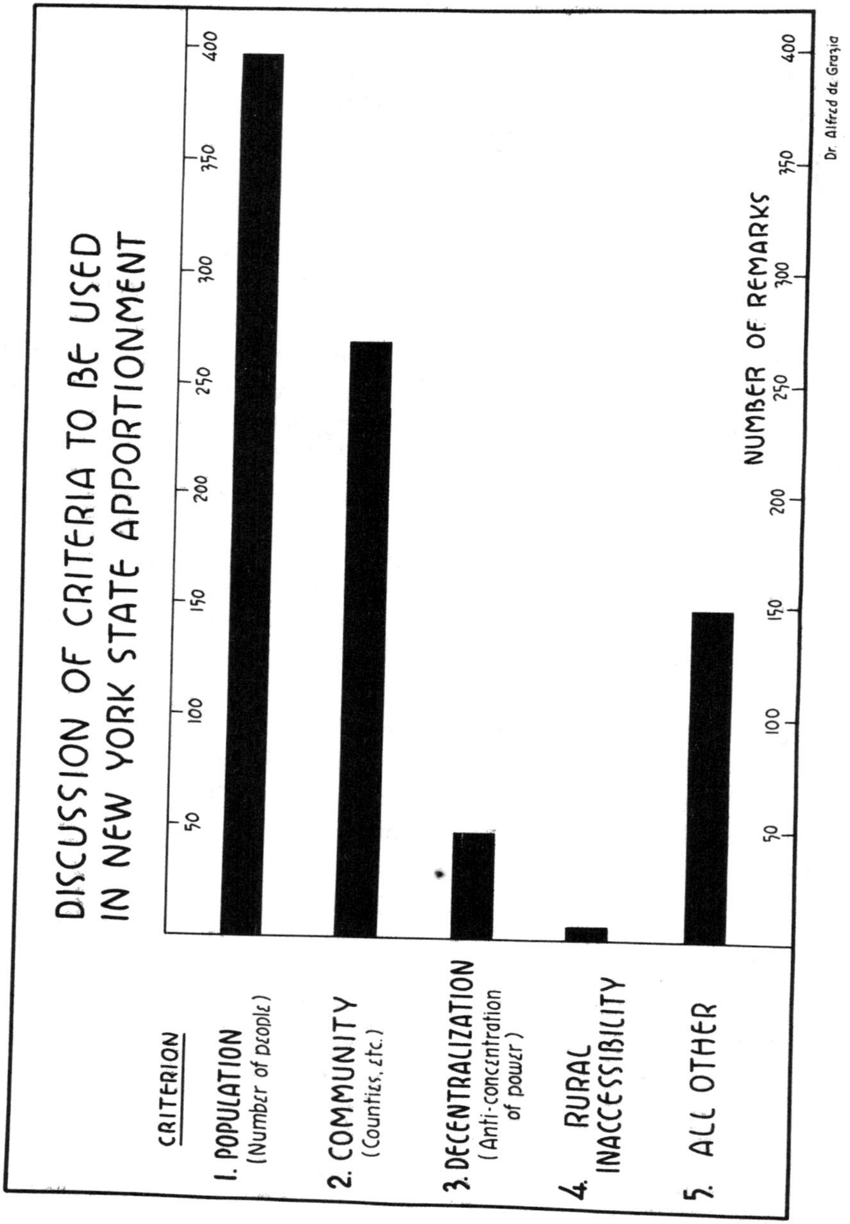
DISCUSSION OF CRITERIA TO BE USED
IN NEW YORK STATE APPORTIONMENT
CRITERION
1. POPULATION (Number of people)
2. COMMUNITY (Counties, etc.)
3. DECENTRALIZATION (Anti-concentration of power)
4. RURAL INACCESSIBILITY
5. ALL OTHER
50
100
150
200
250
300
350
400
NUMBER OF REMARKS
Dr. Alfred de Grazia

3. A third rational intent is present. That is the protection of less easily organized areas from the political power of more easily organized areas (cf. Figure 3). In the New York case, the instances were easy to recognize and the logic must have been compelling. The memory of Boss Tweed lingered and the frightful Boss Croker made his presence felt. A number of American cities have presented the same problem. Politics have changed somewhat in America since then, but not enough to make this motive and the plan to carry it into being much less cogent. The big city presents better opportunities to organize on a large scale than the country and smaller cities do. There can be a boss of a rural area, there can be a county courthouse gang, there can be a clique that runs a small-sized city and all of these present serious problems—but a Chicago or New York machine might dominate a whole State if given the chance and repeat on a State-wide scale what was perpetrated upon their own city.[13]

That is, the constitutional authorities, believing that apportionment was not a matter of atomistic arithmetic but a matter of *general* forces and that therefore the machines of the city might discriminate severely against the country, engaged in *preventive restraining action.*[14]

In numerous realms of life, the law tries to engage in such preventive discrimination in favor of the probably or potentially weaker —laws giving extra assurance of legal defense to the poor; relieving

---

[13] This is a rational fear, if not a demonstrable proposition. Cases of State-wide machines emanating from a large city are rare, perhaps because of the apportionments in effect. "Some compromise with the principle of exact equality is clearly desirable in this situation, for if Chicago were to receive its full share of members in the State legislature it would virtually control all legislation." E. Durfee, "Apportionment of Representation in the Legislature," *University of Michigan Law Review* (1945), 1093. The big city delegations rarely act as units, but it is true that their only possibly unifying force is organized party control. There is no point where "democracy" becomes "machine domination," of course; there is only a gradual upswing in organized power with the expansion of seats. Cf. Charles S. Hyneman, *Illinois Law Review,* September-October 1951, 544.

[14] Cf. below p. 127 where the cube law of majorities is discussed.

the poor from burdens that the well-to-do have to carry; providing educational opportunities to the poor; cutting down the estates of the rich deceased; giving minorities representation regardless of numerical proportion in committees of legislative bodies and elsewhere; laws against tendencies to monopoly; laws giving minority elements some kind of "better deal," as labor unions are helped to organize within corporations.[15]

In the apportionment formulas for the State of New York, we see this motive not only in written documents and the history of city-state relations, but also statistically manifested in the workings of the formula, where an additional slight skewing of the proportionality of representatives to population occurs in the largest urban centers in discrimination or weighting, and more specifically of course in the rules of apportionment that no county may have more than one-third of the representation in the Senate (no county has ever achieved this population status) and no adjoining counties are permitted more than half the seats. (Ten states have similar limits.)

Furthermore, this same goal has another side to it. That is the doctrine of checks and balances. As with the Federal Government and many States, the New York State representative system was intended to prevent one single interest in the society or government from gaining ascendancy over another.

It must be pointed out that this weight, aside from the never-achieved absolute limits, has been quite slight when motives of population proportionality and local community representation have been allowed for. It has not been permitted, whatever the fear of machine domination of the State was and is, to play more than a small part in the actual apportionment formula. To determine whether the actual distribution of seats in an assembly can be reconciled with an underlying set of motives, I devised the formula contained in Figure 4 and its explanation. A weight was given in the equation to each factor of concern to the constitutional authorities and to the degree of the concern. Then the apportionment afforded to each county by the equation is matched with the

---

[15] Cf. R. G. Dixon, Jr., "Legislative Apportionment and The State Constitution," *Law and Contemporary Problems* (Summer 1962), 360-66.

Figure 4

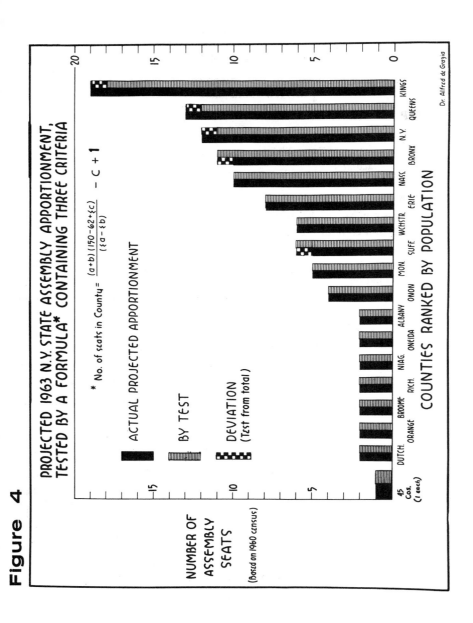

PROJECTED 1963 N.Y. STATE ASSEMBLY APPORTIONMENT,
TESTED BY A FORMULA* CONTAINING THREE CRITERIA

$$* \text{ No. of seats in County} = \frac{(a+b)\ (150-62+\Sigma c)}{(\Sigma a - \Sigma b)} - C + 1$$

ACTUAL PROJECTED APPORTIONMENT

BY TEST

DEVIATION
(Test from total)

NUMBER OF
ASSEMBLY
SEATS

(based on 1960 census)

COUNTIES RANKED BY POPULATION

Dr. Alfred de Grazia

* * * * *

Explanation of Figure 4

A Test of Rationality in Apportionment, Adjusted for Application
to New York State Assembly

STEP

1. $X = \dfrac{(a - b)\,(150 - 62 + \Sigma c)}{(\Sigma a - \Sigma b)} - c + 1$

2. Test: $\dfrac{\text{actual } x}{x}$ must be between 1.25 and .75

Where

1. X is number of seats of County A
2. "1" is weight of the *community factor*
3. "a" is the citizen population of County A
4. "b" is the citizen population of County A or 108,272 (average district population of New York State) whichever is less
5. "Σa" is the total counties' citizen population (that is, State citizen population)
6. "Σb" is "b" for all counties
7. "150 — 62" = Total Assembly Seats less 1 for each of 62 counties
8. "c" = 1 for every 1,000,000 citizen population of County A or major fraction thereof in excess of 1,000,000 (the *anti-centralizing factor*), i.e., $\dfrac{a}{1,000,000}$ which means the quotient of the division less the decimal part of the quotient
9. "Σc" = "c" for all counties (10 in 1960)
10. The *modalizing* (population equalizing) factor is inherent in the distribution of 88±c seats according to population of the counties
11. The final test is designed to provide for an *allowance* of 25% of the difference between the actual situation and the test result. This allowance is for *uncontrollable technical factors* such as changes in the population between apportionments, unused fractions, and a minimal malapportionment. This allowance is not used up in any county. In the case of Suffolk County, with the biggest relative deviation of any, the actual seats are one less than the test formula assigns, or 5/6, or .83.

* * * * *

actual proposed apportionment for 1963. It is evident that the actual apportionment of the New York Assembly is a close reflection of a constitutional theory that gives prominence to population, some emphasis to community, and a weight against overcentralization of power. Other formulas might have been devised, basing their weights on slightly different judgments of the constitutional rationale. But any one of them would be a far cry from the wholly inadmissible pretense in practically all statistics of apportionment, which set up only the equal-populations motive and compare that with the actual apportionments. And what has been done here for New York could be done for every other State in the Union and with the Congress.

4. Still another motive has played a part in the creation of the apportionment formula. This has been the belief that it is physically easier to represent people densely concentrated in a city than the same number scattered throughout the countryside (see Figure 3). Every candidate for public office in the country who has been stuck in the mud or snow while canvassing will say amen to this weight given to smaller numbers.[16] One New York State Senate district is larger than the State of Connecticut.

More important, perhaps, is the availability of multiple sources of conveying opinions and desires in a densely settled area. The mass media, the offices of government, and the offices of many of

---

[16] If one were to examine a map showing the location of Ford car dealers, or of a life insurance company, or to plot locations of wholesalers of wrapping papers, he would probably find that these, like many other companies and governmental agencies maintain offices doing less volume in rural and small city areas' than other offices in big cities. It is unlikely that these companies carry on disproportionate expense because they are dominated by the rural or small town customer. They justify their activity by making more money with more offices doing less volume. More city business can be transacted through a single office than town and country business. The work of legislators is in good part liaison and broker between individual constituents, groups, and governmental units on the one hand and the agencies of the State on the other. The town and country legislator cannot transact the volume of business a city legislator can. (Incidentally, some allowance is made in various legislatures for extra help for city legislators to carry their heavier volume of work.)

47

the utility and other corporations of a quasi-public character are more accessible in a city. Resort to politicians is probably less required and less employed. This is only one kind of representation, to be sure, but it has to be considered.

The possibilities of further weighting are myriad, and a great many, both "good" or "bad," would be rational notwithstanding. Territory; population numbers; contiguity; compactness; periodicity; conformity to census; community boundaries; natural communities; balance of power; anti-monopoly; individualism; partisan concentration or dispersal; functional groups; age concentration; terrain; ideologies; race; ethnic background; religion; voting participation; and other criteria used to discriminate in other devices of representative government, can also be used to discriminate in apportionment. Why not give smaller constituencies to representatives from poor areas on grounds that their people have more problems of the type the government can solve, a weighting incidentally that would set both parties to increased activity in the poorest areas of the State.[17] Whatever the goodness of the results, the device would be rational. No doubt some of the force and eagerness behind the nationwide drive to reapportion is the feeling of groups concentrated in poorer areas that their strength might be enhanced; yet the opposition may be similarly motivated by a feeling that it itself is *already* the poorer group. It is poorer in its capacity to organize for action in the legislature and poorer economically.

Suppose a legislature or constitutional convention decides it is more important that a greater number of people vote than that they vote in equal-population districts. (Many reasons might be advanced of partisan kind, of a philosophical order, of educational or fiscal nature, etc.). This is not a hypothetical question because in principle it is what happens when seats are apportioned, say, on the basis of votes cast in the average of the last four elections. This too would be rational.

National surveys have discovered that relatively fewer residents of large cities know the name of their Congressman than town and

---

[17] Cf. below Figures 7 and 8, where it is shown that this actually is done in Tennessee and elsewhere.

country residents.[18] Does this indicate a greater need for such legislative representation in outlying districts and justify more legislators per capita?

We might weight intelligence and known performance in civic affairs as shown by voting, attending meetings, answering tests on politics, and so on. Such of these weightings as have been tried have not been overthrown because they were irrational but because of a sweeping prejudice against them. Modern social science can just about do anything with surveys and maps of the State.

But all the good ideas in the world cannot be adopted. Perhaps it may be as well to let the constitutional authorities have the last say, even if they are not so flamboyant and imaginative and use different kinds of rationality in thinking and action and are not so fully rational, and even if they settle down with only the motives of population, community, and political anti-concentration contained in their apportionment.

5. Unquestionably a fifth motive played a part in the devising of the Senate apportionment in New York and other States. This is reflected not in the weighting, but in the size of the Senate. The basic size of 50 is set small in order to promote deliberation and close relations among the Senators. One by-product, perhaps relatively insignificant, is that apportionments that take into account community and population are rendered more difficult because of the small number of seats to distribute over a large State of 62 counties. Again the scheme is rational, even though it may arbitrate against community representation in order to allow for more equal populations. It may be observed that the smallest communities of a State apportioned by community have a cause for complaint in being grouped into a district with other communities; the smallest counties are often so joined. They are as underrepresented by the

---

[18] American Institute of Public Survey, March 1942: Question: "Do you happen to know the name of the Congressman from your district?" Percentage who knew name: Farmers 67%; Residents of towns under 10,000 pop., 61%; Residents of cities over 500,000, 23%. Cited in V. O. Key, Jr., *Public Opinion and American Democracy* (New York: Knopf, 1961), 494.

community criterion as the populous counties are by the *population* criterion.

6. A final miscellaneous group of elements may contribute unavoidably to discrepancies in the exact loading of an apportionment, or may be minor elements that can only be sensed qualitatively. Such would be rules to forestall gerrymandering, to follow administrative boundaries, to run along rivers, and to use up fractions of population. Once it is decided to do more than engage in the apportionment geometry of strictly equalized populations, larger remainders and more irregular districts become almost inevitable.

To conclude the discussion of rationality, it may be well to examine a second case. The State of Tennessee came under fire in the case of *Baker* v. *Carr*[19] for supporting an "irrational" system of apportionment. Our logic thus far does not permit us to agree with the opinion of at least one Justice on the matter. Justice Clark felt that a necessary part of the idea of rationality was regularity and uniformity of treatment of electoral districts. He applied a statistical index to the Tennessee apportionment and found a large number of "unexplainable" irregularities. A "crazy quilt without rational basis," he called it. Districts of equal populations had different ratios of representatives and some districts of lesser population had higher ratios of representatives than larger districts. Justice Harlan commented upon Justice Clark's index and amended it, in a way that improved its validity; he did not, however, commit himself to this method of determining rationality.

We used the Clark-Harlan index to plot the Tennessee case on a graph and, as expected, there occurred the irregularities referred to by the Court (Figure 5). To show that by this index of "rationality," another State's apportionment might be said to be "rational," I plotted the New York State district ratios on the same graph, using the same index. It can be observed that the New York apportionment, by this notion of rationality, is considerably more rational than the Tennessee one. In New York, seats per county rise constantly as county population rises. In Tennessee, many a county has less seats than a county of smaller population.

---

[19] 369 U. S. 186 (1962).

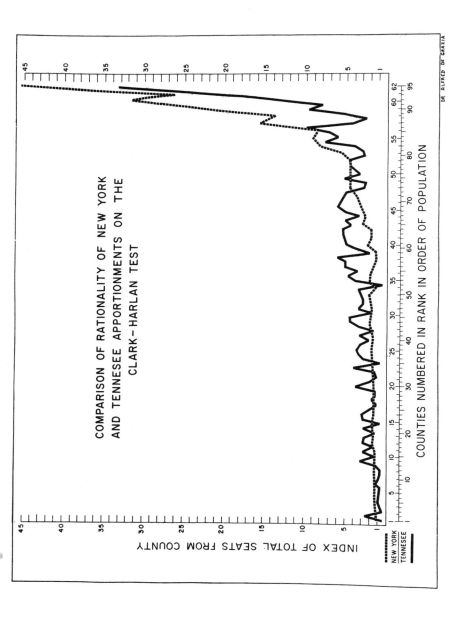

COMPARISON OF RATIONALITY OF NEW YORK
AND TENNESSEE APPORTIONMENTS ON THE
CLARK–HARLAN TEST

INDEX OF TOTAL SEATS FROM COUNTY

COUNTIES NUMBERED IN RANK IN ORDER OF POPULATION

NEW YORK
TENNESSEE

DR ALFRED DE GRAZIA

Explanation of Rationality
Test Using the Clark-Harlan Formula to
Compare Tennessee and New York Total
Representation

1. Both Houses of Tennessee and New York are covered by this formula.

2. The formula is that proposed and used by Justice Clark in *Baker* v. *Carr* and amended by Justice Harlan. Justice Clark indicated that he regarded this as a test of the rationality of an apportionment system and that the Tennessee apportionment failed to satisfy the test.

3. The formula is computed as follows:

Using the more numerous house as the base, a multiplier was calculated for the Senate. Thus: Tennessee has 99 Representatives and 33 Senators. 1/99 = 1/33 x 3. Three is the Tennessee multiplier. If a county had 3 Representatives and 1 Senator, its *Index of Total Representation* was 3 + (1 x 3) or 6. The same was done for New York, where the multiplier is 2.6. When a county had less than one Assemblyman or Senator, its population was calculated and divided into the total district population for that Senator. For example, Chautaugua County in New York State has 1 Assemblyman and shares a Senator with one other county. The total population of the district is 210,150 which is divided by the county population (135,190). The resulting fraction is then inserted into the formula, thus: Chautaugua = 1 + (.6 of total district population x 2.6) = 2.56.

4. The Tennessee index is multiplied by two, to make it visually more comparable to the New York index.

5. FINDING: The uniformity of the New York State apportionment is clearly manifest in this comparison with the Tennessee apportionment termed irrational by Justice Clark. In several places, the New York chart dips as a result of the division of seats into fractions, but this phenomenon is of minor importance in the total picture of uniform progression.

6. As is stated in the text, the idea of rationality represented in this formula is almost exclusively "equal-populations," and does not reflect the ideas of the constitutional authorities of either State.

However, further reflection and study has persuaded me that the idea of rationality used to judge the Tennessee case is incorrect by the logic of rationality earlier advanced, and also dangerous. For one thing, it assumes that an electoral district and the people in it are the same, and that there must be regularity of treatment for the groups into which people fall just as for individual persons themselves. If the Tennessee legislature, or any other State legislature, operating under the authority of its constitution, decides to apportion each seat individually it may be quite rational. It may examine the individual local case, and in the light of general criteria for the State as a whole as well as the needs of the locality, assign to a seat a constituency characterized by a variety of traits—economic, social, political, geographic, and demographic. If afterwards, the seats are plotted by population and a great irregularity is shown, it is just one more proof that all in life that is good is not uniform. We are not possessed of the evidence to show how the Tennessee apportionment came about—we know of enough to feel it may be strongly criticized—but with all its irregularity it might still be the most rational and best apportionment in the country.

We conclude in general that in apportionment rationality is an ensemble of different permissible motives incorporated in a set of devices to assign seats to various groupings of a population. Any concept other than this would be as "arbitrary and capricious" as the arbitrary and capricious action it set out to exclude and nullify.[20]

Equality and Numbers Magic

A second common concept in apportionment with ideological overtones' is equality. What is rational may still be inequitable, and what is inequitable may be unconstitutional. First we discuss the

---

[20] Professor McCloskey asks (*op. cit.,* 63) what "judicially discoverable and manageable standards" as recommended by the Supreme Court (Baker v. Carr, 217) are; he says "that issue, *mirabile dictu,* is not treated at all in the opinion of the Court. One sentence suffices to dismiss it: 'Judicial standards under the Equal Protection Clause are well developed and familiar, and it has been open to courts since the enactment of the 14th Amendment to determine, if on the particular facts they must, that a discrimination reflects no policy, but simply arbitrary and capricious action.' "

idea of equality, and then take up the associated ideology of numbers. Following thereafter is the discussion of the majority principle, which has been declared to be associated with the idea of equality in apportionment.

The date of the first cry for equality is shrouded in prehistory. The cry has been taken up by countless tongues over the millennia, and we cannot believe that anything that we say here is going to still the din, either by satisfying it or drowning it. The variety of meanings of "equality" in discussions of apportionment alone must be in the dozens. Let us look at the matter theoretically, at first, because only thereby can the babel be translated and myriad facts be ordered.

When somebody is equal (or unequal) to somebody else or to a group of others, he may be equal (or unequal) in many ways: in apportionment, when somebody is equal (or unequal) to others, he may be equal (or unequal) also in many ways. Suppose he were made equal in all of these ways of apportionment. He would have to be sure that he was not thereby and at the same time being made unequal in other valued ways. That is, assuming it were possible to make a man equal to other men in the working of a device of apportionment, he would perhaps not be happy if he were to become unequal in some other way having only an indirect bearing upon apportionment or resulting from equality of apportionment. For example, in the Soviet Union, the introduction of "equal suffrage" between women and men was accompanied by a loss of power to both with regard to their leaders; that is, they became more unequal to their leaders. Sometimes the gaining of equality in one sphere is caused by the same underlying source as the increase in *inequality* in another sphere. The Soviet instance just cited is again apropos. Communism basically incorporates these contradictions of equality. A systems approach to the study of apportionment and representative government is needed. By its terms before introducing a change into the system we have to be sure how the system works, and then that the change will produce most of its intended effects and also not produce undesirable, unintended effects.

54

A second distinction can be made, treating of the confusion that has arisen between the use of the term "equal" in apportionment and the term "equal protection of the laws." The fact that the word equal appears in both contexts means little in logic or evidence. There is a great chasm between the two terms that can be bridged solely by evidence showing that certain kinds of unequalness that must be shown to exist in the apportionment system produce certain other conditions that have been condemned by the Constitution and courts to be illegal according to the term "equal protection."[21] It is unfortunate that the similarity of the words causes a great many people to jump to the conclusion that the facts underlying both situations must be the same. Actually, a better term, logically and statistically, for the advocacy of equal-population districts would be "modal," for modal refers to whatever is the most common value or trait under discussion. The equal-populations advocates then are seeking to modalize the vote in the apportionment formula (and also to equalize it). Equality is impossible (because of leftover fractions, etc.), but the districts can be strongly modalized. And the perjorative bias of the word "equal" would be reduced. But there is little hope that we shall be permitted this reasonable language.

In the hypnotic glare of the "equal-protection" idea, blindly seeking a grotesquely simple equality, the argument against the existing apportionments continues to run: if the number electing an official in one constituency is less than in another, when both officials have the same formal power in the same policymaking group, then the people of the first constituency are denied something (are unequal) and the extent of the denial and inequality varies with the difference in numbers between the two constituencies. Practically all of the literature on apportionment consists of a reiteration of this argument in highly colored language and the presentation of lists of figures "proving" the inequality. No attention is paid to whether people are truly represented. The representation of a single individual is assumed to depend upon how many people share his vote for the same official. The only factor the studies pay attention to

---

[21] Dixon, *loc. cit.*

in apportionment is equality of the district populations. The many other factors that compose the representative system are not attended to.

Rare exceptions include the encyclopaedic Robert Luce (*Legislative Assemblies, Legislative Principles,* and *Legislative Procedure*), who is made uneasy by equal-districts agitation, though he is the compiler of a mountain of documentation. Thomas Page knows that all is not well but finally gives over to the tide (*Legislative Apportionment in Kansas*). Bebout is concerned (See below p. 124). Jewell is not a devout enthusiast (*Politics of Reapportionment,* Part I, 28, 44 *et passim*). Others may be anxious about the nonrational ideological configuration that envelops the problem of apportionment but find their anxiety difficult to express. This is to be expected, by the nature of ideology. Sindler has observed this; he comments briefly:

> Many themes meriting serious exploration have tended to go by default, being caught between the extremist simple standard of those against malapportionment and the general inarticulateness of those on the other side. For example, the concept of area representation, taken by itself or as the medium for minority interest representation, has no less solid a place than the population principle in democratic values. If the contemporary reliance on counties poorly satisfies the rationale underlying area representation, perhaps more effort should be devoted to devising better methods of implementing the principle and less to discarding it.[22]

Several law review commentators (Neal, McCloskey, Friedelbaum, and Dixon) are alerted and anxious, rather more over the excesses of judicial power than over the flowing force of the political doctrines involved.

The judges appear in some cases to be seized by the equality compulsion, in others to be perturbed over the expansion of jurisdiction. Both commentators and judges must rely upon the poor and biased diet of fact fed in through the scarce empirical studies as predigested by illy-prepared legal counsel on both sides of the issue.

---

[22] Allan P. Sindler, "Baker v. Carr, How To 'Sear The Conscience' of Legislators" *Yale Law Journal,* # 1 November 1962, 29.

With two or three exceptions, there appears to be an almost complete failure of the judicial process as an intelligence system.

It is not clear where the "right of equal district populations" comes from. It has only a relative historical authority. It cannot come from the Federal Government, where we find the Electoral College, the Senate, and a House of Representatives largely or partly organized under contrasting principles. Perhaps from something called "equal representation" but little attention is paid to this concept either, except that propagandists say it too is exclusively authoritative. There is no clear indication of what behaviors of legislators will be changed if seats are "equalized." A mechanical view of man and human relations is held and a "numbers obsession" evolves.

It is finally a belief in the magic of numbers; equal numbers are better magically than unequal numbers. As an idea that moves men, the slogan of equality is a fact. As a description of an accomplished relation existing among or between men, it is almost always one of the most limited ways conceivable for describing how and why men are acting as they do. That is, as a description of social behavior, it is almost always nonsense. Society is made up of men who behave unequally in politics, and representation is made up of thousands of relations. Equal representation is not a specific set of behaviors grouped around the color of a man's skin, or a religious group, or a college. It is a highly general set of responses.

To repeat the argument advanced, again in stripped-down form, "equal representation" is whatever happens when everyone in the State is the same fraction (e.g., 1/100,000) of whatever constituency he belongs to for casting his vote. "Fairly close to the same fraction," some will add, realizing immediately that no man can draw boundaries around exactly equal populations. Somewhat close, they say, because they also realize that population groupings do not reflect citizen groupings, nor citizen groupings voter groupings, nor voter groupings participating groupings. But the measure of "somewhat close to the same fraction," as, for example, 1/100,000 and

1/90,000 and 1/110,000 are somewhat close, must not wander farther from the ideal lest the quality of democracy be strained.[23]

What does happen when Citizen Jones has a fraction of 1/100,-000 and Citizen Smith one of 1/150,000? The propaganda for the theory of equal representation says Jones has one and a half times as much power over his representatives as Smith does.[24] This is, of course, entirely fictional. The best social scientists are desperate to establish by prolonged research the parameters of the power of one man in relation to another in their personal relations. They would be aghast at the problem thus phrased in the political arena. What the proponents of "equality" must be saying about effects of unequal representation (if we are to take them seriously) is that when a goodly number of heavily populated districts of one kind of people have the same number of legislators as a goodly number of thinly populated districts, some people of the former have less power over the latter than they would have if they obtained more legislators.[25] Therefore they appeal to their numbers.

Probably they would not appeal nearly so strongly if they did not believe that considerable differences existed between themselves and the others, and therefore the problem of apportionment arises when people feel unrepresented in certain actions of the State government or officials and search for a way to redress the balance. Since those

[23] It is amusing to note that the venerable New Hampshire Constitution (Part II, Article 26) provides: "And that the state may be equally represented in the Senate, the legislature shall, from time to time divide the state into twenty-four districts, as nearly equal as may be without dividing towns and unincorporated places; and in making this division, they shall govern themselves by the proportion of direct taxes paid by the said districts."

[24] Many cases can be adduced to prove this point. Here is one: "Under the present apportionment, it takes only 65 second-ratio county voters to equal the power of 100 first-ratio county voters . . . etc." David Wells, *Legislative Representation in New York State* (1962), 18.

[25] Cf. H. D. Lasswell and A. Kaplan, *Power and Society* (New Haven: 1950), for a careful logical use of the term "power" in this sense, and an explanation of its meanings and implications. A has power over B when A can influence the X policies of B.

who are agitating are thinking primarily of their own views being forwarded, it is not to be expected that they would give much thought to whether new forms of unrepresentation would occur for many of their neighbors. It is a distinct likelihood that at any given moment, nearly half the people out of the minority who have any opinion on an issue in a given district differ from the other half in that opinion, including the issue of apportionment.

Consequently, it must be said that the meaning of "equal representation" is in large part fictional and rhetorical, and in minor part an expectation that from districts of equal population having equal numbers of representatives will come certain changed behaviors arising in fact not from the inequalities of representation but from the location of those inequalities. That is, if two districts are of the same social composition and outlook, it would make little difference to anybody except those who obtain jobs and favors on a personal basis whether they have equal representation, but since they are likely to have different views, then they should be kept in equality of representation.

We note then that what is wanted, as usual, is more power for one's own interest and less power for an opposing interest, and the slogan of equal representation is one of many slogans standing for different instruments of achieving a more favorable position in the eternal struggle for valued goals that mark the political process. As such it does not achieve the status of constitutional authority, a term to be defined fully in Chapter 7.

We may apply this theory to an example. If a search is made of the New York State system of apportionment for those qualities that make it in large degree a popular government, responsive to opinions on local matters as well as general matters, we do not have far to go. Every voter in New York can cast a vote that is weighted the same as every other vote for the election of Governor and other high State offices, provided of course the election system is efficient and honest, and provided that a number of strangely apportioned situations are accepted in the system of governing political parties and nominating those officers, and provided that he does not mind the plurality principle snatching all seeming power from his vote if as much as one person more votes for a candidate opposing his own. The decision of the Liberal Party officers, for example, on supporting or not supporting a major party candidate can do much more to change the weight of his vote than he and all his co-constituents can do if they voted as one man. The same voter can cast a vote of the same weight as all other voters in his district in electing a legislator whether Senator or Assemblyman. This much seems to satisfy most people.

But it does not satisfy others. I turn to the brief of the plantiffs in *WMCA* v. *Simon,* the New York legislative apportionment case of August 1962 for anoth?r example. Following the brisk trade in identical types of figures over the past 50 years or so, they calculate and submit statistics such as the following:

County	Citizen Population	Senators	Assemblymen
New York	1,795,726	6	16
Bronx	1,378,181	4	12
Kings	2,595,187	9	22
Queens	1,484,214	5	13
Suffolk	261,003	1	3
Nassau	655,690	3	6

In contrast to the foregoing, the following upstate counties were represented as follows:

50th Senate District			
Ontario	59,269	—	1
Schuyler	14,066	—	1
Seneca	28,254	—	1
Wayne	56,662	—	1
Yates	17,461	—	1
Total	175,712	1	5

It is apparent from the foregoing that whereas one Senator represents approximately 299,000 citizens in New York County . . . one Senator represents substantially fewer citizens, in some instances almost as few as half as many citizens in upstate counties.

60

Strangely enough, almost no other evidence save material of this character is given for the allegations of plaintiffs in this and other cases concerning the disparate voting power of city and rural citizens. The New York petition goes on to say that "gross distortion exists with respect to both houses of the New York legislature. For example one Assemblyman represents 17,461 citizens of Yates County; one Assemblyman represents approximately 115,000 citizens in Bronx County." It is said that these are "merely illustrative" of the malapportionment. One wonders why it was not stated that these were several extreme cases and why averages of different types, such as averages of the four quartiles, were not produced, as well as tables.

Of course, this deficiency is made up to a certain extent in the supporting affidavits, which, true to form of political science in this field, heavily belabor the obvious, namely that the big cities of the States have larger constituencies than the small cities and country. This is scarcely a fact at issue. Elaborate statistical exercises of this kind only serve to exaggerate one aspect of a highly complex and variable situation. About these other matters, the plaintiffs in the various apportionment cases around the nation have little to say.

Their statistics, of course, do not lie. But they are one-sided and misleading. For example, there is a repeated recourse, already alluded to, to extremes of the biggest centers and the smallest. The New York plaintiffs gloss over the fact that New York State *as a whole* is very urban, that upstate New York which is Republican is just about as urban as Democratic downstate New York.[26]

We can go directly to one of the strongest pamphlets put out by the advocates of reapportionment in New York, and written by Mr. David Wells of the ILGWU, and make from any one of several tables that are supposed to show the terrible disparity between the cities and the country a much less extreme picture.[27] Suppose we take from the whole New York State population 100 persons at random; using the figures offered us, we can report on their probable repre-

[26] Ralph Straetz and Frank J. Munger, *New York Politics* (New York: 1960).

[27] *Op. cit.*

sentative condition in respect to the weighting of their vote for the Assembly. Of these 100 sampled persons, 74 will probably be from districts that have an average of 130,000 people in them, while 9 will come from districts averaging 110,123 persons. It is unlikely that these 83 people will feel very different from one another, and they may not even notice those privileged 17 who come from districts averaging only 62,765 people. That is to say, the vast majority of people in New York State come from districts of about the same size. The vast majority have a modalized vote, even by the improper absolute test proposed by the WMCA plaintiffs. So far as the average size of districts in the same county is concerned, taking the State as a whole, the average deviation of those counties that are supposed to be underrepresented is about 20 percent, those over-represented about 40 percent. Actually the terms "overrepresented" and "underrepresented" are also question-begging terms, which, like "equal representation," served the goals of the New York plaintiffs.[28] They might just as well say even while subscribing to their equal populations belief, that the vast majority are simply represented, the others more or less privileged.

Although, as it appears, we are sceptical of the factual basis for determining that votes are unequal when a purely arithmetic test is applied, we are certain that a system that is quite "unequal" in the Constitutional sense by *any* test can be detected and disqualified. It would be a system that allows no popular majority to accumulate and have legal or other compelling effect under any circumstances. That is to say, representative government can operate without majority rule, and operate very well. Indeed, it is the usual practice. But a majority sentiment of the people has to be able to dig itself through the representative institutions of government, to wit, through the top executive and through the legislative branch, if the American republican and representative government is to be said to exist, or, if you will, if the equal protection of the

---

[28] Cf. Ralph M. Goldman, "A Research Program on Apportionment," I *American Behavorial Scientist, PROD,* September 1957, 18, where Professor Goldman enters a plea for more objective use of terms in writings on apportionment.

laws is to be guaranteed to the people. If the means of constitutional amendment is by popular majority or if the means is within reach of elected officers, or of a referendum to the public, then a large weight would additionally have to be given the system for fulfilling the conditions of representative government. Thus it is that when one is for "equality," even in a limited sense as here, he can only give it some positive impact by translating it into some form of majority rule. And that is why the doctrine of equality is politically and constitutionally dangerous. Even when we include it among our favored doctrines, we must appreciate that its applications can produce endless inequalities.

The Majority Principle

How can the idea of equal-population districts be reconciled with the idea of majority rule? We have stated that the history of struggles over representation is marked by one form of thought— the egalitarian-majoritarian—that demands both with fervor. Are they not inconsistent? If X, Y, and Z are three constituencies and each has 1,000 people and one representative, then, according to this belief, each person living in X, Y, and Z has equal power over his representative, and representatives A, B, and C have equal power in relation to each other in respect to whatever they do collectively and individually as legislators. (All other factors in the representative system are held constant in order for this statement to be examined on its own merits.) However, if the election of A, B, and C is by majority principle then a number of people will not be "equally powered"—they will win or lose all. Furthermore, if A, B, and C have to decide by majority vote (as legislatures usually try to do), then it will occur that A and B, or B and C, or A and C can override the third man. The majority principle operates to make a great many people and representatives greatly "unequal" all the time.

Why, if the majority principle wreaks such havoc on it, does the equal-populations principle of apportionment fascinate so many people, including many scholars? For one thing, it leads a life of its own; people think about politics and government in simple, separate compartments of the mind. Secondly, it has the magic of the term "equal" to take the sting from the majority dictate. And it has the "true" effect of perhaps bringing about changes that the equal-population advocates desire, regardless of principle. Another reason suggests itself. There is a widespread psychological feeling, inherited from history, that the mass of people is discriminated against; if the mass, which is the great majority, could gain *equality* and act by its *majority* against the enemies of the people, it would arrive at *Truth* and mass happiness. Rigid leveling of people to the status of numbers is deeply and psychologically associated with both advocacy of the masses and the desire to dominate them. True mass leaders of equality movements almost always aim at dictatorships. This view and desire are also associated with a closed-minded belief that truth-on-earth exists and is known. Historically it has never wanted more than a slight shift of emphasis to have this truth become the exclusive possession of the leader or an elite. The majority principle, as dogma, is seen as the next best thing to unanimity, even autocracy. It is common in Greek, Roman, and European history—even world history—for the Caesars, Napoleons, Mussolinis, and Lenins to be preceded by the dogmas of equality and right of the majority. The leader then becomes the head of the majority on its way to absolute rule. The German sociologist, Max Weber, once said of this type of "democracy," it is a political system in which people elect a leader whom they trust, whereupon the elected one obtains the right to impose on people and parties the most absolute silence.[29] To give way to a belief in the sacred significance of numbers, in apportionment as elsewhere, permits the justification of ever stronger rule in the name of the majority principle.

---

[29] M. Weber, *Max Weber: Ein Lebensbild* (Tubingen, 1926), 429.

4.

APPORTIONMENT PRACTICES AND REAPPORTIONMENT

APPORTIONMENT HAS BY NOW been defined, but reapportionment requires clarification. We call a revision of any substantial kind in an apportionment system, "reapportionment." A reapportionment that is completed with a substantial deviation from the formula prescribed for it by law is called malapportionment. Also included under malapportionment is a failure to carry out a basic constitutional requirement to reapportion.

65

There is little doubt that a flagrant contradiction between law and practice, such as exists between the legally stipulated criteria of apportionment and the actual apportionment in a number of American States, causes moral uneasiness and discontent. It is one thing to say that any apportionment system favors some interest or attitude over another, and quite another thing to assert that every kind of manipulation of apportionment is merely another way of accomplishing this fact, and has no important moral consequences.

American State legislatures, which in this way scarcely vary from many other legislatures elsewhere, have often relied upon rotten boroughs and gerrymandering to preserve the existing proportions of seats or to increase the proportion of seats held by a single party or faction. Rotten boroughs are historical accidents that give disproportionate weight to the votes of a thinly populated district in relation to a thickly populated one, despite a rule requiring reapportionment. New York State, for example, has population disparities among districts, as prescribed by law, and therefore these are not rotten boroughs. The American Senate is not a rotten borough because it was never supposed to be based on the principle of equal populations. But rotten boroughs are found in American States, the legislatures of which have failed to carry out mandatory periodic reapportionments in order to adjust the size of districts to population changes. The most populous lower house district in Indiana, for example, was in 1961 nearly six times the population of the smallest district, owing to the legislature's failure since 1921 to carry out the apportionment procedure prescribed in the State Constitution, which calls for equal-populations districts.

Gerrymandering, on the other hand, is a positive act of malapportionment. It is a violation or evasion of the law or tradition or consensus. Its special character emanates not from being a biased apportionment (for all apportionments are "biased"), but from its disharmony with the legal order. Any system of apportionment may be gerrymandered, although some systems, such as the free apportionment of proportional representation, are more difficult to gerrymander than others.

The gerrymander most commonly observed in American politics understandably affects the prevailing system of apportionment by territorial survey. In North Carolina, for example, one finds certain long bacon-like strips that slice up the Republican vote into pieces manageable by the dominant Democrats. A territorial gerrymander may violate the stipulated condition that district populations be equal or that district boundaries be drawn solely with reference to enclosing a contiguous and compact area and population or both. The usual objective of a gerrymander is to maximize the number of districts returning safe majorities for the apportioning group and to minimize the number of districts returning safe majorities for the opposition party or faction.[1] The gerrymandering group seeks to draw district boundaries in a way that will concentrate its opponents' votes in as few districts as possible and will spread its own dependable majorities over as many districts as possible; or it seeks to disperse the majorities of its opponents and gather together its own partisans to create new majorities. Hence the success of a gerrymander depends upon an accurate knowledge of past voting behavior in the various constituencies and a reliable prediction about voting behavior in the future in both old and new constituencies.

The temptation to gerrymander or encourage rotten boroughs is always present in a legislature. Extreme gerrymanders, maximizing the predictive ability of the dominant faction, are usually prevented not only by various legal provisions but also by the erring legislators' consciences that provide generally some modicum of shame and by their fears of exciting too great a popular resentment against transgressions of traditional and legal rules. The gerrymander and rotten boroughs are perversions of the accepted traditional and legal order, it is well to emphasize here, and can be distinguished readily from the more general struggle to achieve social values, of which the process of apportionment forms part.

---

[1] Other motives can inspire gerrymanders, as when a powerful member of the legislature "pulls rank" and gets approval of a district specially tailored to his needs. Of course, the line between gerrymanders and a great many "tailored" variations is frequently a matter of quantity, not of motive.

Nor are the debates in legislatures over the different mathematical techniques of accomplishing apportionments of the same moral stature. It is known that difficulties occur in apportioning seats to any legislature in which the number of seats is fixed. In the American Congress, for example, heated argument has arisen over the problem of assigning each State the proper quota of seats from the fixed number available. What to do with the surplus votes in each State that simple arithmetic division leaves standing is the crucial question. At least five different techniques can be used: the method of smallest divisors, of the harmonic mean, of equal proportions, of major fractions, and greatest divisors.[2]

Each technique of apportionment benefits some States and hurts others. But the point here is that disagreement over the technique to be chosen, although it exhibits often the same play of interests as is displayed in debates over gerrymandering or the general criteria of apportionment, is on a different plane of values. For here, even given a principle of apportionment to which all would agree if they could, mathematical social science cannot provide an exact formula in accord with the principle. Such disagreement, therefore, may be regarded as a legitimate contest, to be tolerated as morally different from the contests occurring over malapportionment and the criteria for basic apportionment.

A major problem of reapportionment centers on keeping legitimate disagreements within bounds. When legislators are responsible directly for reapportionment, they tend to enlarge the scope of dispute beyond the inevitable minimum. Hence reapportionment is increasingly being entrusted to less involved personnel. Among them are included the constitutional prescription of the apportionment itself, the constitutional prescription of the exact criteria and timing of apportionment; the standing legislative enactment that is quasi-self-executing; the standing legislative enactment that permits

---

[2] W. F. Wilcox, "Last Word on the Apportionment Problem," and L. F. Schmeckebier, "The Method of Equal Proportions," in XVII *Law and Contemporary Problems* (1952), 290, 302 and cf. Schmeckebier, *Congressional Apportionment* (1941).

the executive to apportion if the legislature fails to take action; the initiative and referendum; the political executive apportionment under constitutional or legislative authority; and the nonpolitical administrative apportionment or judicial apportionment under constitutional or legislative authority. All these techniques deny with reason that the legislature's conscience will suffice in all cases to provide a necessary reapportionment according to established and accepted criteria. In line with the view that responsibility in politics should be continually thrust upon its appropriate bearers, it seems best to give the legislature the original initiative, recurrent periodically, to carry out constitutional directives to apportion, and then only thereafter to legislature-related bodies. Executive power should not, for it need not, be enhanced by being charged with apportionment. Judicial power, if employed, should be severely limited by legislation. Such is the logic of the separation of powers.

Considering the infinite variety of apportionment systems that is possible, the federal apportionment system, the 50 State systems, and the half million or so other apportionments in local and administrative government in the country are remarkably similar. Practically every known technique of apportionment is used somewhere in America, but the vast majority of jurisdictions are grouped around fundamental homogeneities.

Chart I presents the major variables and methods used in the State systems. It reveals that with eight exceptions the State Constitutions make some provision for community interests to be expressed, and all arrange for seats to be distributed in some minimal sense at least in accord with population. Professors Gordon E. Baker and Malcolm E. Jewell provide the following summary of provisions on apportionment in the States, which emphasizes a distinction between population-base and boundary-base plans (See Table I). There are as they point out, many cases in between, using both principles, and there is no "pure equal-population plan," if only because the constitutional authorities and legislators are overwhelmingly persuaded that district lines should have some relation to other existing communities and jurisdictions. *(Text continued on page 83)*

Chart I.

APPORTIONMENT OF LEGISLATURES

As of December 1962

State or other jurisdiction	Citation: article and section of constitution	Basis of apportionment — Senate	Basis of apportionment — House	Frequency of required reapportionment — Required every 10 years*	Frequency of required reapportionment — Other schedules for reapportioning	Apportioning agency	Dates of last two apportionments
Alabama	IV, 50; IX, 197-203; XVIII, 284	Population, except no district more than one member.	Population, but each county at least one member.	X	......	Legislature.	1962 1901
Alaska	VI, XIV	Area, with population factors; combination of house districts into four at-large districts and a varying number of minor districts.	Population (civilian) 19 districts.	X	......	Apportionment board; its recommendations are reviewed, and confirmed or changed by the Governor.	1956 1953
Arizona	IV, 2, 1 (1)	Districts specifically established by constitution.	Votes cast for Governor at last preceding general election, but not less than if computed on basis of election of 1930.	..	After every gubernatorial election (every 2 years).	No provision for Senate; redistricting for House by County Boards of Supervisors.	1958 1956

State							
Arkansas ... VIII, 1-5; Amndt. XLV	Senate is fixed. (a)	Each county at least one member; remaining members distributed among more populous counties according to population.	X	......	Board of Apportionment (Governor, Secretary of State, and Attorney General). Subject to revision by State Supreme Court.	1961	1951
California ... IV, 6	Population, exclusive of persons ineligible to naturalization. No county, or city and county, to have more than one member; no more than three counties in any district.	Population, exclusive of persons ineligible to naturalization.	X	......	Legislature or, if it fails, a reapportionment commission (Lieutenant Governor, Controller, Attorney General, Secretary of State, and Superintendent of Public Instruction). In either case, subject to a referendum.	1961	1951
Colorado ... V, 45-47	Population ratios.	Population ratios.	..	Every 5 years (b)	General Assembly.	1953	1933
Connecticut . III, 3, 4, 5	Population, but each county at least one member.	Two members from each town having over 5,000 population; others, same number as in 1874.	Senate	......	General Assembly for Senate, no provision for House.	H-1876 S-1903	1818 .....
Delaware .. II, 2	Districts specifically established by constitution.	Districts specifically established by constitution.	..	......	No provision.	1897	.....

Chart I. continued

APPORTIONMENT OF LEGISLATURES

As of December 1962

State or other jurisdiction	Citation: article and section of constitution	Basis of apportionment — Senate	Basis of apportionment — House	Frequency of required reapportionment — Required every 10 years*	Frequency of required reapportionment — Other schedules for reapportioning	Apportioning agency	Dates of last two apportionments
Florida	VII, 3, 4	Population, but no county more than one member.	3 to each of 5 largest counties, 2 to each of next 18, 1 each to others.	X	......	Legislature.	H-1955 1945
Georgia	III, 2; (Par. 1), 3 (Pars. 1, 2)	Territory, but no senatorial district more than one member.	Population, i.e., 3 to each of 8 largest counties, 2 to each of next 30, 1 each to others.	X	......	General Assembly "may" change senatorial districts. Shall change House apportionment at first session after each U.S. census.	1961 1953
Hawaii	III, 2, 4	Districts specified by constitution.	Population, but each county at least one.	X	......	Governor.	1959 1958

State	House	Senate			Authority	Recent	Prior
Idaho .....III, 2, 4, 5; XIX, 1, 2	One member from each county.	Total House not to exceed 3 times Senate. Each county entitled to at least one representative, apportioned as provided by law.	X	......	Legislature.	1951	1941
Illinois ....IV, 6, 7, 8	Fixed districts based on area.	Population.	House	Senate is fixed.	General Assembly or, if it fails, a reapportionment commission appointed by the Governor.	1955	1901
Indiana ....IV, 4, 5, 6	Male inhabitants over 21 years of age.	Male inhabitants over 21 years of age.	..	Every 6 years.	General Assembly.	1921	1915
Iowa ......III, 34, 35	Population, but no county more than one member.	One to each county, and one additional to each of the nine most populous counties.	X	......	General Assembly.	H-1927 S-1911	1921 1906
Kansas ....II, 2; X, 1-3	Population.	Population, but each county at least one.	..	Every 5 years.	Legislature.	H-1961 S-1947	1959 1933
Kentucky ..Sec. 33	Population.	Population, but no more than two counties to be joined in a district.	X	......	General Assembly.	1942	1918

73

Chart I. continued

APPORTIONMENT OF LEGISLATURES

As of December 1962

State or other jurisdiction	Citation: article and section of constitution	Basis of apportionment		Frequency of required reapportionment		Apportioning agency	Dates of last two apportionments
		Senate	House	Required every 10 years*	Other schedules for reapportioning		
Louisiana	.. III, 2-6	Population.	Population, but each parish and each ward of New Orleans at least one member.	X	......	Legislature.	1921 1902 `
Maine	...... IV, Pt. 1, 2, 3; IV, Pt. II, 1	Population, exclusive of aliens and Indians not taxed. No county less than one nor more than five.	Population, exclusive of aliens. No town more than seven members, unless a consolidated town.	House(c)	......	Legislature.	H-1961 1955 S-1961 1951

74

State	Const.	Basis (1)	Basis (2)			By whom apportioned		
Maryland	..III, 2, 5	One from each county and from each of six districts constituting Baltimore City.	Population, but minimum of two and maximum of six per county. Each of Baltimore districts as many members as largest county.(d)	..	.....	Membership frozen for House; no provision for Senate.	1962	1943
Massachusetts	..Amdt. LXXI	Legal voters.	Legal voters.	X	.....	General Court.	H-1947	1939
							S-1960	1948
Michigan	..V, 2-4	Districts specifically prescribed by constitution.	Population.(e)	House	Senate is fixed.	Legislature or, if it fails, State Board of Canvassers apportions House. Senate is fixed.	1953	1943
Minnesota	..IV, 2, 23, 24	Population, exclusive of nontaxable Indians. (f)	Population, exclusive of nontaxable Indians.(f)	X`	And after each state census.	Legislature "shall have power."	1959(g)	1913
Mississippi	..XIII, 254-256	Prescribed by constitution.	Counties grouped into three divisions, each division to have at least 44 members.	X	.....	Legislature "may."	1916	1904

Chart I. continued

APPORTIONMENT OF LEGISLATURES

As of December 1962

State or other jurisdiction	Citation: article and section of constitution	Basis of apportionment Senate	Basis of apportionment House	Frequency of required reapportionment Required every 10 years*	Other schedules for reapportioning	Apportioning agency	Dates of last two apportionments
Missouri ...III, 2-11	Population.	Population, but each county at least one member.	X	.....	House: Secretary of State apportions among counties; county courts apportion within counties. Senate: by commission appointed by Governor.	1961 1951
Montana ...V, 4; VI, 2-6	One member from each county.	Population, but at least one member from each county.	X	Session following federal census.	Legislative Assembly.	1961 1951
Nebraska ...III, 5	Unicameral legislature—population excluding aliens.		..	From time to time, but no oftener than once every 10 years.	Legislature "may."	1935 1920
Nevada ...I, 13; IV, 5	One member for each county.	Population.	X	.....	Legislature.	1961 1951
New Hampshire Pt. II, 9, 11, 26	Direct taxes paid.	Population. (h)	House	Senate—from time to time.	General Court.	H-1961 1951 S-1961 1915

New Jersey .IV, ii, 1; IV, iii, 1	One member from each county.	Population, but at least one member from each county.	X	. . . . . .	For lower house, Governor apportions among counties; Secretary of State certifies to county clerks.	1961 1941
New Mexico IV, 3	One member from each county.	At least one member for each county and additional representatives for more populous counties.	X	. . . . . .	Legislature "may."	1955 1949
New York ..III, 3-5	Population, excluding aliens. No county more than 1/3 membership, nor more than 1/2 membership to two adjoining counties.	Population, excluding aliens each county (except Hamilton) at least one member.	X	. . . . . .	Legislature. Subject to review by courts.	1954 1944
North Carolina .II, 4-6	Population, excluding aliens and Indians not taxed.	Population, excluding aliens and Indians not taxed, but each county at least one member.	X	. . . . . .	General Assembly.	H-1961 1941 S-1941 1921

Chart I. continued

APPORTIONMENT OF LEGISLATURES

As of December 1962

State or other jurisdiction	Citation: article and section of constitution	Basis of apportionment — Senate	Basis of apportionment — House	Frequency of required reapportionment — Required every 10 years*	Frequency of required reapportionment — Other schedules for reapportioning	Apportioning agency	Dates of last two apportionments
North Dakota	II, 26, 29, 32, 35	Set by constitution. but somewhat reflects population.	Population, but each county or district entitled to one member.	X	.....	Legislative Assembly, or if it fails, a special board composed of Chief Justice of Supreme Court, Attorney General, Secretary of State, and Majority and Minority Leaders of House shall reapportion House.	1961 1931
Ohio	XI, 1-11		Population, but each county at least one member.	X(i)	Each biennium(i).	Governor, Auditor, and Secretary of State, or any two of them.	1961 1951
Oklahoma	V, 9-16	Population	Population, but no county to have more than seven members.(j)	X	.....	Legislature.	1961 1951

State							
Oregon ....IV, 6, 7	Population.	Population.	X	......	Legislative Assembly, or failing that, Secretary of State. Reapportionment subject to Supreme Court review.	1961	1954
Pennsylvania II, 16-18	Population, but no city or county to have more than 1/6 of membership.	Population, but each county at least one member.	X	......	General Assembly.	H-1953 S-1921	1921 1906
Rhode Island ...XIII; Amdt. XIX	Qualified voters, but minimum of 1 and maximum of 6 per city or town.	Population, but at least one member from each town or city, and no town or city more than 1/4 of total, i.e., 25.	:	......	General Assembly "may", after any Presidential election.	H-1930 S-1940	....
South Carolina .III, 1-8	One member from each county.	Population, but at least one member from each county.	X	......	General Assembly.	1961	1952
South Dakota ..III, 5	Population.	Population.	X	......	Legislature, or failing that, Governor, Superintendent of Public Instruction, Presiding Judge of Supreme Court, Attorney General, and Secretary of State.	1961	1951

79

Chart I. continued

APPORTIONMENT OF LEGISLATURES

As of December 1962

State or other jurisdiction	Citation: article and section of constitution	Basis of apportionment — Senate	Basis of apportionment — House	Frequency of required reapportionment — Required every 10 years*	Other schedules for reapportioning	Apportioning agency	Dates of last two apportionments
Tennessee ..II, 4-6		Qualified voters.	Qualified voters.	X	......	General Assembly.	1962 1901(k)
Texas ......III, 25-26a, 28		Qualified electors, but no county more than one member.	Population, but no county more than 7 representatives unless population greater than 700,000, then 1 additional representative for each 100,000.	X	......	Legislature or, if it fails, Legislative Redistricting Board (Lieutenant Governor, Speaker of House, Attorney General, Comptroller of Public Accounts, and Commissioner of General Land Office).	1961 1951
Utah ......IX, 2, 4		Population.	Population. Each county at least one member, with additional representatives on a population ratio.	X	......	Legislature.	1955 1931

State	Basis of apportionment — House	Basis of apportionment — Senate	Senate	Senate—or after each state census.	Body which reapportions		
Vermont ...II, 13, 18, 37	Population, but each county at least one member.	One member from each inhabited town.			Legislature apportions Senate; no provision for House.	H-1793(I) 1962	 1941
Virginia ...IV, 43	Population.	Population.	X	......	General Assembly.	1962	1958
Washington. II, 3, 6; XXII, 1, 2	Population, excluding Indians not taxed and soldiers, sailors, and officers of U.S. Army and Navy in active service.	Population, excluding Indians not taxed and soldiers, sailors and officers of U. S. Army and Navy in active service.	X	......	Legislature, or by initiative.	1957	1931
West Virginia ..VI, 4-10, 50	Population, but no two members from any county, unless one county constitutes a district.	Population, but each county at least one member.	X	......	Legislature.	1950	1940
Wisconsin ..IV, 3-5	Population.	Population.	X	......	Legislature.	1951	1921
Wyoming ..III, 3; III, 2-4	Population, but each county at least one member.	Population, but each county at least one member.	X	......	Legislature.	1931	1921
Guam ......Organic Act: 1950 (2d), Sec. 512	Legislature elected at large.					....	....

81

Chart I. continued

APPORTIONMENT OF LEGISLATURES
As of December 1962

State or other jurisdiction	Citation: article and section of constitution	Basis of apportionment — Senate	Basis of apportionment — House	Frequency of required reapportionment — Required every 10 years*	Frequency of required reapportionment — Other schedules for reapportioning	Apportioning agency	Dates of last two apportionments
Puerto Rico.	III, 3, 4, 7	Two senators for each of eight senatorial districts, and eleven at large.	One representative for each of 40 representative districts and eleven at large.	X	......	Board composed of Chief Justice and two additional members representing different political parties, appointed by Governor with Senate consent.	1952 1917

* Every ten years, or after each federal census.

Abbreviations: H—House; S—Senate.

(a) Amendment adopted November, 1956, "froze" the senatorial districts as then established. Future apportionment of the Senate will not be made.

(b) Required every five years, after each federal and each state census.

(c) Constitutional provision "at most ten years and at least five."

(d) In 1948, membership in House frozen at then existing levels.

(e) Any county with a moiety of ratio of population is entitled to separate representation.

(f) Section on Indiana is still in constitution but is ineffective due to federal legislation.

(g) Effective in 1962.

(h) Amendment adopted in November, 1942, sets the membership of the House of Representatives at not more than 400 and not less than 375. It requires, for each representative additional to the first, twice the

number of inhabitants required for the first, with the provision that a town or ward which is not entitled to a representative all of the time may send one a proportionate part of the time, and at least once in every 10 years.

(i) At the reapportionment following the decennial census, a ratio is established to provide for fractional representation during the succeeding decade. Any county or senatorial district with a population larger than the minimum requirement for Representative or Senator, but not as large as required for an additional full Representative or Senator, is allotted fractional additional representation by adding a Representative or Senator for one to four of the legislative sessions during the decade.

(j) In practice no county has less than one member.

(k) In 1945 a flotorial district was changed to eliminate one county.

(l) Apportionment plan for House is provided in the constitution with no provisions for reapportionment. House apportionment thus dates from adoption of constitution in 1793.

Source: Book of the States, as amended to December 1, 1962.

TABLE I.

STATE LEGISLATIVE APPORTIONMENT

Basis	Senates	Houses	Total
Population (including 1 Unicameral)	19	12	32
Population, but with weighted ratios	1	7	8
Combination of population and area	17	28	45
Equal apportionment for each unit	7	1	8
Fixed constitutional apportionment	4	1	5
Apportionment by taxation	1	0	1
	49	49	99

Source: Gordon E. Baker, *State Constitutions: Reapportionment* (New York: National Municipal League, 1960), 5.

The community interest is least provided for in the constitutions of the States of Indiana, Nebraska, Oregon, South Dakota, Tennessee, Virginia, Washington, and Wisconsin. The population idea is least facilitated by the formal law in the States of Georgia, Arizona, Arkansas, Florida, and Rhode Island.

Ease of Change

An important theme in the legal rhetoric of reapportionment is that the difficulty of change can justify court intercession. Developed in the opinion of the Court in *Baker* v. *Carr,* it is carried forward in the literature and other court opinions. Since judicial logic is not for ordinary mortals, we are not permitted to say that the courts have made this idea law, but we should examine the idea for its larger meaning and on the chance that it is sidling into the law. Some change in the system of apportionment and also reapportionment is everywhere made possible, if only by constitutional amendment. In a number of cases, the change, even by formal requirement, is difficult to bring about. Nevertheless the difficulty of formally changing the apportionment system and reapportioning is not manifested sharply in such cases as Georgia, Florida, and Rhode Island.

What makes formal change difficult or easy is one or a combination of factors. The agencies that must make the change would be

83

the victims of change also. The Constitution itself may be difficult to amend. The exercise of the power to change is permissive, not mandatory. And there may be no public demand.

The Georgia Constitution, contrary to the supposition of many, is not difficult to amend. How difficult is difficult? The Federal Constitution requires a two-thirds vote of both Houses of Congress or a convention summoned on petition of two-thirds of the State legislatures to propose an amendment. It requires ratification either by the legislatures of three-fourths of the States or conventions in three-fourths of the States. By contrast, the Georgia Constitution is amended by a proposal of two-thirds of the members of both houses of the legislature and ratification of the proposed amendment by a majority of electors voting thereon, at the next general election. (The 1945 Georgia Constitution scarcely changes the procedure of previous Constitutions.) The number of amendments to the Georgia Constitution exceeds those to the Federal Constitution several times over. Furthermore, the Georgia amending procedure is typical of American States. Every State save New Hampshire provides that the legislature may initiate the proposal. Some require more, some less than a two-thirds vote of the legislature. Almost half the States require a second approval of the amendment in two successive legislative sessions; Georgia is not among them. Georgia is one of the majority of States that require ratification by a majority voting on the proposal. Some States make ratification more difficult. Thirteen States permit a popular initiative on proposals to amend their constitutions, which proposals are then submitted to popular referendum. We are led to conjecture now. If the typical method of amending State constitutions should be federally unconstitutional, so must be the method of amending the Federal Constitution itself. But the Supreme Court cannot declare the Constitution of the United States unconstitutional. Or can it? It might certainly imply such by declaring unconstitutional the imitative or even more easily amended constitutions of a number of States. This is absurd; that it can even be implied by analogical reasoning from the activity of the judiciary

(Text continued on page 92)

CHART II
RECENT CHANGES IN STATE AND FEDERAL APPORTIONMENT

I. STATUS OF FEDERAL APPORTIONMENT

A. CURRENT U.S. HOUSE SEATS

B. STATES WHICH GAINED SEATS

C. STATES WHICH LOST SEATS

D. STATES WITH NO CHANGE[a].

E. FUTURE NUMBER OF SEATS (1963 -1973)

F. STATES WHICH APPROVED CONGRESSIONAL APPORTIONMENT AND / OR DISTRICTING BILLS IN 1961 OR 1962 (AS OF NOVEMBER 6)

G. STATES WHICH GAINED A SINGLE CONGRESSIONAL SEAT UNDER APPORTIONMENT BUT DID NOT REDISTRICT, FORCING AT - LARGE ELECTION OF ADDITIONAL SINGLE MEMBERS IN 1962.

II. STATE APPORTIONMENT AND DISTRICTING ACTION[b].

A. STATES WHICH APPROVED STATE APPORTIONMENT AND / OR REDISTRICTING SINCE 1959 FOR ONE OR BOTH HOUSES.

B. SOURCE OR INITIATION OF RECENT STATE APPORTIONMENT AND / OR REDISTRICTING ACTION.

1. BY LEGISLATIVE ENACTMENT

2. BY ADMINISTRATIVE OFFICERS OR COMMISSIONS

3. BY STATE AND FEDERAL COURT ORDER (STATES WHERE APPORTIONMENT LAWS HAVE BEEN STRUCK DOWN AS UNCONSTITUTIONAL.)

a. DEADLINE SET FOR ENACTMENT BY LEGISLATURE

b. REFERRED DECISION TO A REFEREE OR SPECIAL COURT MASTER

c. IMPOSED ITS OWN SPECIFIC APPORTIONMENT PLAN

C. RECENT RELEVANT CONSTITUTIONAL AMENDMENTS, PROPOSITIONS, ETC.

1. ADOPTED BY VOTERS

2. REJECTED BY VOTERS

CATEGORY FOOTNOTES FOR CHART II
"Recent Changes in State and Federal Apportionment"

a. None of these States chose to redistrict in the two years following announcement of the 1960 census results. (In a November 1960 referendum, however, North Dakota voters approved a congressional districting bill dividing the State into two districts in place of the previous at-large election of the State's two House members.)

b. Data are based upon reports in the national press, telephone conversations, and correspondence with State officials around the country, and information in the following publications:

William J. D. Boyd (ed.), *Compendium on Legislative Apportionment* (New York: National Municipal League, 1962).

Legislative Reapportionment in the States: A Summary of Action Since June, 1960 (Chicago: The Council of State Government, 1962).

"Congressional Redistricting: Impact of the 1960 Census Reapportionment of House Seats" (Washington: *Congressional Quarterly*, No. 39, Part II, September 28, 1962).

Reports in *National Civic Review* (New York: National Municipal League, January 1961—November 1962).

c. There may be several contradictions between the dates of court actions and the dates of the last apportionments noted on Chart I, "Apportionment of Legislatures." These occur because a court order to apportion is not necessarily coincident in time with the implementation of reapportionment.

EXPLANATORY FOOTNOTES FOR CHART II
"Recent Changes in State and Federal Apportionment"

1. Alabama was stymied on redistricting and finally adopted a unique double-primary elimination system in order to reduce the congressional delegation from nine to eight seats.

2. Arizona allowed a redistricting law to go into effect which had been passed by the State legislature in 1947, in anticipation of the State's receiving a third House seat.

3. State Representative Welborn Daniel said on June 2, 1961, that population was only one of several factors considered in creating Florida's compromise congressional redistricting bill. "Other facts include affinity of interest and the number of governmental units such as county commissions and the number of cities with which the Congressman has to deal. The philosophy never has been that population is the only factor." ("Congressional Redistricting: Impact of the 1960 Census Reapportionment of House

Seats" [Washington: *Congressional Quarterly*, No. 39, Part II, September 28, 1962], p. 1622.)

4. Maryland approved a redistricting bill, but it was placed in abeyance by a successful referendum petition. Since the State's congressional apportionment was changed by the addition of only one seat, the sole result was to preserve old districts and force election of a single member at large in 1962.

5. Efforts to create a new congressional district were abandoned by the Republican-controlled General Assembly. Two developments reportedly convinced Republicans that a new district was unnecessary or inadvisable: the death of George H. Bender, a former Representative and Senator, who had broken with the State Republican organization and announced his candidacy for an at-large seat in 1962; the opposition of Republican Representative Clarence J. Brown and other incumbent Congressmen, to the proposed redistricting plans.

6. In its 1961 session, the legislature enacted bills which reapportioned Assembly seats.

7. The legislature revised the distribution of unit votes and the county unit system on which primaries are based, but took no action with respect to legislative reapportionment.

8. The legislature adopted a constitutional amendment which would alter the geographic boundaries of two districts. The amendment needs the approval of the electorate.

9. Senate reapportionment by a State board was passed subject to a referendum which was not initiated.

10. A federal court declared a 1961 Oklahoma reapportionment law null and void and gave the State legislature until March 8, 1963 to reapportion itself. If no reapportionment measure has been enacted by then, the court will reapportion either by some judicially devised formula or by an election at large.

11. Reapportionment measures were voided by a federal court. The court declared that the legislature failed to reapportion on the basis of population. A proposed constitutional amendment also was voided.

12. Proposals for amendments must pass both houses by 2/3 majority in 1963 before going to a popular vote.

13. Delaware's legislature has approved reapportionment that will go into effect if the next legislature also approves.

14. A constitutional amendment passed by the legislature and approved by a federal court was rejected by the voters on November 6, 1962. The court reserved the right to take further action if the amendment was not approved.

87

15. In 1961 the Iowa General Assembly reapportioned the Senate. The legislature also initiated a constitutional amendment which would give more senatorial seats to the more populous counties. The amendment must be passed by the General Assembly in 1963 and then approved by the voters in order to become effective.

16. Although the Kansas House of Representatives was reapportioned in 1959, there has been no significant reapportionment of the Senate since 1939. A State court suit asking that the State Senate be ordered reapportioned has been postponed by agreement of both parties until the legislature can take up the question in 1963.

17. Senate redistricting was passed in May 1960. It partly reduced urban "overrepresentation," Plans for redrawing House lines were dropped.

18. Voters rejected a reapportionment plan approved by the State legislature which would have strengthened the rural position of the State Senate, although giving urban areas more seats in the lower house.

19. The relevant sections of the Missouri Constitution are self-enforcing and require no supplementation. Therefore, there has been no legislation on apportionment.

20. An amendment adopted on November 6, 1962 provides for a combined population-area formula.

21. The lower house was reapportioned. A federal suit has been brought to force reapportionment of the State Senate.

22. Despite challenges to apportionment, it remains in doubt whether the legislature will act. Its hesitancy rests on a ruling by the State Supreme Court that apportionment of Senate seats on the basis of direct taxes paid was "admittedly unique" but not unconstitutional.

23. A reapportionment measure enacted by the Oregon Legislative Assembly in 1961 was declared unconstitutional by the Oregon Supreme Court. The court directed the Secretary of State to draft a reapportionment of Senators and Representatives which was subsequently sustained.

24. At the January 1962 session, a resolution was passed proposing an amendment to the State Constitution relating to the composition of the House of Representatives. This measure must be passed by another General Assembly and then submitted to the electorate for approval or rejection.

25. Unable to enlarge the 30-member Senate without a constitutional amendment, a bill was passed which transferred one seat from Rutland County to Chittenden County (the most populous county).

26. The 1962 West Virginia legislature approved an amendment which was submitted to the voters in November and rejected by a large majority. It would have given the legislature authority to arbitrarily assign at least one House member to each county, regardless of population size.

27. The Wisconsin Senate passed an extraordinary measure July 21, 1962, to reapportion the State by resolution. The plan is designed to realign the State Senate and Assembly districts without the signature of the Governor. The measure would not become effective until 1964 and embodies redistricting provisions vetoed by the Governor earlier.

28. The State Supreme Court overruled the apportionment made by the State Board of Apportionment and issued its own reapportionment of House seats.

29. The courts have ruled that the present apportionment of the State Senate is constitutional and that the State House of Delegates was unfairly apportioned in favor of rural areas. The ruling has led to a temporary reapportionment, giving Baltimore and other large metropolitan areas 79 of 142 members in the lower house.

30. State Supreme Court declared permanent area districts for State Senators unconstitutional. A ruling that the State Senate had to be immediately reapportioned by population was stayed by Supreme Court Justice Potter Stewart pending further disposition of the case by the U. S. Supreme Court.

31. In its decision of June 13, 1962, the Court of Common Pleas gave notice "that constitutional apportionment is a matter that can be adjudicated if the legislature fails to do so." *(Legislative Reapportionment in the States: A Summary of Action Since June 1960 op. cit,* 41.)

32. A federal court ruled that if voters rejected the constitutional plan on the November 6, 1962 ballot, then "further appropriate action can be taken by the court and jurisdiction will be retained for that purpose." *(New York Times,* September 6, 1962, 21.)

33. A three-judge federal court gave the Georgia Legislature until the end of 1962 to reapportion in compliance with constitutional standards.

33b. The courts are threatening action if no reapportionment efforts are made by the legislature in 1963. *(National Civic Review,* September 1962, 441.)

34. The legislature was given until November 24, 1962 to reapportion itself.

35. A federal court has retained jurisdiction.

36. The federal court said it is retaining jurisdiction and will take action if the 1963 session of the State legislature fails to act.

37. A federal court declared a 1961 Oklahoma reapportionment law null and void and gave the State legislature until March 8, 1963 to reapportion itself. If no reapportionment measure has been enacted by then, the court will reapportion either by some judicially devised formula or by an election at large.

38. A State court warned that failure to reapportion both houses of the legislature during the 1963 session would lead to further action by the court.

39. The court decided to give the General Assembly of Tennessee an opportunity at its 1963 session to enact a fair and valid reapportionment. The court retained jurisdiction, and the case may be reopened after June 3, 1963 upon application of any party or upon the court's own motion.

40. In January 1962, the State Supreme Court refused to pass upon the validity of Wisconsin's apportionment, but did state that it would consider a new suit if the legislature should fail to act by June 1, 1963.

41. Appointment of a court master to reapportion is threatened. No legislative action was completed.

42. Since the North Dakota Legislative Assembly did not adopt a re-apportionment during the 1961 legislative session, the duty to reapportion fell upon a five-man board. The group's plan was held unconstitutional. The North Dakota Supreme Court ruled that it was therefore the legislature's responsibility to reapportion.

43. Involved litigation in Wisconsin has produced no action. The special master, in a preliminary report to the federal court, said that present legislative districts do not deny any constitutional rights of voters as charged by the State Attorney General. Court action was halted August 2, 1962, due to failure of the State to pay a $3,500 federal court fee.

44. Two alternatives were on the November 1962 ballot in the form of constitutional amendments. The one receiving the most votes won.

45. Georgia voters approved an amendment on November 6, 1962, for the selection of State Senators on a countywide basis in counties where there is more than one senatorial district. This provision contradicts a State court ruling that State Senators should be elected only by voters in their respective districts.

46. A constitutional amendment to increase the size of the House of Representatives was defeated by the voters in 1948; a similar measure was approved by the voters in 1960.

47. Voters approved by 311,586 to 231,329 an amendment on November 6, 1962 providing for House reapportionment by the Speaker on the basis of population in the case of 20 seats, all other seats going one to each of the 100 counties. (Data in a memorandum from the Secretary of State of North Carolina.)

48. North Dakota voters on November 8, 1960, approved, by a vote of 133,523 for and 109,377 against, a referendum proposal dividing the State into two congressional districts in place of the previous at-large election of the State's two House members.

49. An amendment for a three-man commission (the State Attorney General, Secretary of State, and State Treasurer) to handle reapportionment was approved on the November 1962 ballot. The validity of the election result is being litigated.

A proposed change in Oklahoma's constitutional formula for membership in the State House of Representatives was severely defeated on September 12, 1961. In September 1960 approval for a special commission to make apportionments and an increase in the legislature (which would have benefitted the more populous counties) was defeated by a vote of almost two to one.

50. A November 1962 proposal for a constitutional convention in 1965 to alter the legislative organization was approved by a vote of 216,977 for and 206,390 against. (Data received in a telephone conversation with the Secretary of State of Tennessee.)

51. In the 1960 general election, an initiative measure to establish reapportionment of the Senate was rejected by the voters. A constitutional amendment to increase the State Senate from 40 to 50 members was defeated on November 6, 1962. Final unofficial returns indicated a vote of 2,101,810 for and 2,295,323 against. (Data received in a telephone conversation with the Secretary of State of California.)

52. ". . . two proposals were submitted to the voters for reapportionment of the State legislature in recent, times; one at the election of 1954, and another in 1956. These two proposals were dubbed 'Federal Plans' and the heart of them was to apportion the Senate on a more geographical basis (to favor the rural areas) and the lower house on population (to favor the urban areas). Both proposals were soundly defeated at the polls." (Leo C. Riethmayer and Franklin M. Bridge, "Colorado," *Compendium, op. cit.,* 2.)

53. Constitutional amendments dealing with apportionment have been defeated by the voters in 1956, 1958, 1959, and 1962. The most recently rejected constitutional plan called for eight additional Senators and 40 additional Representatives and had been approved by a federal court.

54. In 1960, Iowa voters rejected a proposed Constitutional Convention which had been promoted on the basis of apparent dissatisfaction with the apportionment of the State's legislature.

55. The voters rejected the General Assembly's congressional redistricting plan on the November 6, 1962 general election ballot by a vote of 115,557 for and 211,904 against.

56. In November 1962, the Missouri electorate defeated a proposal to have another Constitutional Convention.

57. A constitutional amendment was rejected by the voters in 1961.

58. An initiative measure for a constitutional amendment on the November 1962 ballot was defeated by an unofficial vote of 199,404 for and

313,682 against. The proposal backed away from making population the main standard. (Data in a memorandum from the Secretary of State of Oregon.)

59. A proposed constitutional amendment regarding reapportionment was rejected by the electorate at the November 8, 1960 election. The legislature reapportioned itself in 1961.

60. An initiative measure for reapportionment on the November 1962 ballot was defeated. The proposal would have given urban areas somewhat more strength in both houses. In the fall of 1958, the people rejected by a vote of 32,579 for and 365,018 against a constitutional amendment that provided for a reapportionment and redistricting commission which would act in case the legislature either failed to redistrict itself after every federal census, or if redistricting legislation was referred to the people and rejected by a referendum vote.

shows the intricate and involved ways in which a prejudice against States such as Georgia can work its way into public law.

Sensing their weakness in this regard, several proponents of equal-population districts have fumbled for a logic that would prove State Senates are not analogous to the federal Senate.[4] Historically their argument is groundless and unworthy of attention. Moreover as a political matter, it seems absurd to assert that the National Government may have a Senate based upon representation of each State equally, but that a State Senate may not be composed of representatives from the counties or multi-county areas of the State. Still, if they wish the courts to destroy the State Senate apportionments, they must chew this rag. Else the courts will preceive clearly that to disturb the structure of State Senates must imply the right to reshape the United States Senate.[5]

An even more radical question here arises: if ease of change is demanded in regards to apportionment, would it not be also mandatory in general? That is, a constitution difficult to amend in one respect must usually and in principle be equally difficult to amend in most other respects. Hence wherever it is difficult to bring change in any area affecting federally guaranteed rights, the factors causing

---

[4] Cf. Robert B. McKay, *The Federal Analogy,* (New York: National Municipal League, 1962).

[5] Cf. Chief Justice Warren in Bolling v. Sharpe, 347 U.S. 497, 500 ". . . it would be unthinkable that the same constitution would impose a lesser duty on the Federal Government."

this difficulty must be nullified. The Federal Constitution might be drastically extended to the amending clauses of all the State constitutions. A principle of constitutional law would then evolve, maintaining that a State amending procedure and indeed a State procedure for political change in general, must always be easy enough to permit to occur whatever the federal courts deem to be necessary changes in State government and society.

It should of course be realized that a constitution that seems difficult to amend at one point in time, appears easier to change at another point. The Federal Constitution has had flurries of amending activity, and authors no longer accuse it of the inflexibility they once thought inherent in it. Furthermore, if some of the testings of public sentiment on systems of apportionment (reported in the final chapter) are considered, it would appear as likely as not that *community representation* plans or *combined plans of the type in use today* would win over *equal-populations* plans, and therefore *these,* not the equal-populations plans, would be the principal beneficiary of easy procedures for change.[6] Indeed, viewing the general structure of power throughout the country, it would appear that *any* test of apportionment plans would tend towards the existing patterns, and the only way to change this general situation is by a naked use of judicial power.

Recent Change

It is questionable whether change in apportionment in America is any less rapid than change in other areas of law—say, insurance regulation, sexual morality, race relations, tax reform, or municipal planning. It takes 5½ years to try the average accident case in Illinois courts. Is this or some other measure of "reasonable speed" relevant? It should be noticed that it may take about 18 months following a decennial apportionment before the figures are in for many apportionments and before the legislature is called into session, studies the districts, debates the matter, and concludes the legislative process. Meanwhile the population changes.[7]

---

[6] See below, Chap. 6, pp. 138-139.

[7] Professor Ernest Reock of Rutgers University has shown by fairly complicated projections that an average for populations of districts during the

What does Chart II show to be the history of changes in apportionment? In the last three years reapportionment has been very frequent. Twenty-eight States approved State apportionment or redistricting bills for one or both houses, 22 by legislative action, four by administrative agencies or commissions and two by court-imposed plan. Five additional legislatures passed bills, but by law had to submit them to a new legislature and referenda. In seven States reapportionments were adopted by voters.

Twenty-one States approved congressional apportionment or districting bills in 1961-62 (as of November 6, 1962). Five of the nine States that gained seats in the Congress following the 1960 census chose not to redistrict and to permit the election of a Congressman-at-large (all single). The 16 States that lost seats redistricted.

Much of this activity has been owing to the assumption of jurisdiction over apportionment by the Supreme Court. However, the year before saw considerable activity, owing partly to the availability of decennial statistics on State populations. Indeed, if we compare the activity in 1961 and 1962 with the activity in 1951 and 1952, we see that in any case, with or without the decision of *Baker* v. *Carr,* the two years after the federal census bring an increase in apportioning work. In 1961-62, 23 States were reapportioned; in 1951-52, 15 States were reapportioned.[8] In 1961, that is, before *Baker* v. *Carr,* 18 States completed reapportionments.[9]

There is no doubt but that the proponents of equal-populations districts whether by change in the system or by legislative action, have received some stimulus from the Supreme Court. In most recent cases the changes have moved toward that doctrine. Professor Reock has indicated that prior to the present time, and going back to the beginning of this century the equal-populations doctrine had

---

whole apportionment period could be used in the decennial apportionment. I doubt that demographic prediction is valid enough to go to this trouble, even granting its value, which I would deny.

[8] In 1953, five States were reapportioned.

[9] Census data for reapportionment was available significantly earlier for 1960 than after 1950.

been losing ground in State apportionments.[10] Still, another factor to be considered here is the increasing pressure from urban sources for increased seats; as the American people have become increasingly urban, urban affairs have colored more and more of State legislative proceedings. Influence follows numbers, with or without formal sanction in the apportionment formula, not only in increasing influence over the Governor, but also over the State offices and over legislators who until lately have represented semi-rural constituencies. Therefore, it is possible that some reapportioning in the direction of equal-populations has come about by the factorial law of political power—influence of a person or group expands by a factor greater than one, from whatever base it may be calculated; and decreases similarly.

Chart II also shows those cases in which apportionment has not occurred in some time, despite State constitutional requirements to the contrary. They number fewer than is popularly supposed. And from these must be taken probably half a dozen States in which reapportionment under court order is imminent, as the Chart shows. It does not show however the States in which excessive gerrymandering is practiced, that is, deliberate malapportionment. Probably only two or three seats in every State are gerrymandered *in flagrante delicto,* which is about the only way in which they may be caught up and chastised by the courts.

---

[10] This would agree with my earlier conclusion about the passing of the crest of the egalitarian apportionment tide (*Public and Republic, op. cit.,* Chap. VI).

95

5.

THE EFFECTS OF APPORTIONMENT

To assess the effects of an apportionment device in the abstract is not easy. No two devices are ever employed under the same circumstances; hence a common method of logical comparison is almost useless. Of beliefs about effects, there are many, as I have shown, and of allegations plenty too, as will be shown here. But for every effect that may be produced by an apportionment device in one setting, a different and even opposing effect may be produced by the same device elsewhere.

It is not surprising therefore that we find quotations such as the following in studies that attempt to deal with effects of apportionment:

> The fact that no simple cause and effect sequence can be ascribed to the influences of the apportionment system does not bear out the claim that the system has no substantive effect on public affairs; instead it indicates that the influences are in most cases subtle and deeply imbedded in the structure of government.[1]

It is most important, of course, that we not be satisfied with merely alleged consequences, and unfortunately, these constitute the vast bulk of material aimed at establishing cause and effect.

Biased Statistics and Semantics

One must apologize for the deficiencies of political science in this regard, too. Practically every study of apportionment made in the last half-century has contented itself with general allegations or has engaged in dubious arithmetic. The arithmetic has rotated its numbers around one premise alone: that equal-populations districts are the sole and ideal test of good representation. The typical study takes up a State or group of States, divides its population by the number of seats in the legislative assembly to get an average, and shows how great are the deviations from the average. Anyone with an almanac, paper and pencil can play this game.

Variations may be introduced, especially if they are biased towards the equal-populations doctrine. Thus Senates and Houses can be added together and an index number can be created. The big counties and the small counties can be separated from the rest and the ratio of members to people can be compared.

The counting can begin with the smallest county and go upward until it is demonstrated that a small proportion of the population can elect a majority of members of the legislature. The counting does not start from the counties of heavy population and move down to a majority, perhaps because it is equally impressive, but in the "wrong" way, to the naive to see how few heavily-peopled areas can run a State. Yet, I know of no study that shows how often districts are lined up in the voting in this way. Professor Carroll Wooddy long ago discovered, on the other hand, that the United States Senate, where the pattern of unequal population districts is

---

[1] William C. Havard and Loren P. Beth, *The Politics of Mis-Representation* (Baton Rouge: Louisiana State University Press, 1962), 77. This painstaking and interesting research study provides abundant material on the traditional political order of Florida and its changes owing to the transformation of the State's population and economy. That it accepts much but proves little about the effects of apportionment does not gainsay its larger merits.

sharply manifested,[1a] rarely votes in a small State vs. big State pattern. Hundreds of papers can be engrossed with statistics on a single State. Still the conclusion can only be the simplest of statements: most jurisdictions are not apportioned by the equal-populations principle.

It must be added that these statistical elaborations of the obvious provide a background for a considerable exercise of evaluative, pseudo-scientific, and question-begging language. The lack of semantic, as well as statistical, objectivity in such studies is remarkable. If they are sincere in these errors, they are not scientists, and if they are insincere, they can be dismissed as propagandists.

Equal-populations advocates, in literature and litigation, are prone to cite the inflammatory language of exceptional persons opposed to their point of view. In the brief of plaintiffs in *WMCA* v. *Simon,* for instance, we find the statement that follows, culled from the proceedings of the New York State Constitutional Convention of 1894:

> I say without fear of contradiction, that the average citizen in the rural district is superior in ˙intelligence, superior in morality, superior in self-government, to the average citizen in the great cities. . . .[2]

The same remark, without its qualification or its subsequent rebuttal, is quoted in a *National Civic Review* (National Municipal League) "report" of New York apportionment news, and in at least two other places in the scholarship of equal-district doctrine. Yet when we go back to the 1894 Constitutional Convention proceedings and do a content analysis of the remarks made there on the subject of city and country, we find a much more temperate setting. Figure 6 presents the facts of the matter. Advocates of city virtues had their day and most of the remarks on both sides were reasonable even in the light of present-day sociology and tastes.

Numerous provincial remarks can no doubt be discovered addressed both to city and country, and every other division of American life. These are not proof of a large and more enduring discrimi-

---

[1a] "Is the Senate Unrepresentative," XLI *Political Science Quarterly* (1926), 219.

[2] U. S. District Court, SDNY, July 1962.

Figure 6

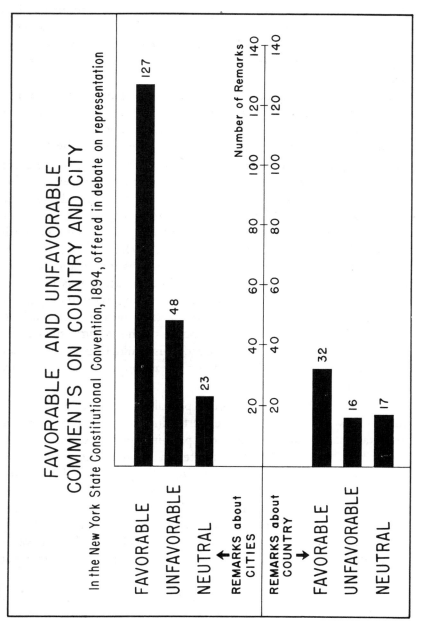

FAVORABLE AND UNFAVORABLE
COMMENTS ON COUNTRY AND CITY

In the New York State Constitutional Convention, 1894, offered in debate on representation

nation. Their citation is not helpful in solving the problem unless their typicality is measured. Moreover, excited *language* is more characteristic of American politics than excited *behavior* is. Nor have American politicians been generally adept at expressing abstract ideas in words. Several intemperate remarks of Gouverneur Morris against the western regions got into Madison's sober and cool notes of the Federal Constitutional Convention in 1789, but they do not destroy the rational motives behind the Constitution or make it invidiously discriminatory, say, against the westerners of the time.

In an effort to find concrete evidences of the effects of different apportionments, I have prepared Chart III. It must be noted that this Chart is based in part upon a volume prepared and published by the National Municipal League. Each State is treated in a couple of pages by a person, often an expert, responding to certain standardized questions. The questions on which the chart is largely based are unsatisfactory. A first leading question asks informants to compute what percent of the minimum 1960 population was necessary to elect a majority of the legislature beginning with the smallest districts. (A pure *ideological statistic* with almost no reference to reality.) The form for each contributor to the volume then asks: "Do the inequities have the effects of discriminating against: (a) either national party? (b) rural or urban populations? (c) any other elements?"

As it stands, the question would probably not be tolerated in a court of law unless posed for expert witnesses with provision for cross-examination, and certainly not permitted in the science of attitude testing, nor even for that matter in an elementary course on political science methodology. An alternative, scientifically permissible, and more productive form would be: "Are they any consequences of the existing apportionment? What are they? What kinds of governmental units, people and groups are given advantages by the existing apportionment? In what way? What kinds of governmental units, people and groups are disadvantaged by it? In what way?"

Still, we are grateful for the existence of this catalogue, and to the many contributors who patiently provided material for it. With

out it, the chart would have been costly and time-consuming to prepare, and the chart does reveal several points of some importance.

Effects on Political Parties

First, those who have sought reform on apportionment to improve
their party's position may be right for their State but wrong for the
Union. Informed opinions seem to indicate that about as many State
apportionments favor Democrats as favor Republicans. Several work
both ways in different parts of the State.

Sometimes accidents benefit one party. By accident is meant that
the basic patterns of party voting behavior concentrate one party's
voting strength in one part of the State that is favored or disfavored
in the apportionment system, without intent; this situation closely
resembles the racial, ethnic, and religious distinctions to be discussed.
Sometimes a shift in party fortunes in the State as a whole, will
produce apportionment legislation that will reverse the effects of
districting upon the formerly favored party. California and Illinois
have seen this occur in recent years.

Now, can we offer any general judgment upon this situation? Any
major change towards equal-populations districts over all the States
will help some big city Democrats in the North and many Republican
suburbs. In the South, the Republicans, who are concentrated in the
cities, will be helped. But much finer analyses are needed in each
State to say more.

More important perhaps than party fortunes will be party-faction
fortunes and the fate of certain kinds of politicians. Extensive shifts
in district boundaries along equal-populations lines will produce
considerable change in the composition of legislatures. The largest
cities in numerous cases will have additional representatives; new
pro-labor union sentiment may be voiced; more non-Caucasian sentiment may be heard; more pro-Catholic and pro-Jewish sentiment
may be reflected. The suburbs, on the other hand, will bring in
opposing sentiments in these regards with their new representation.
In the South, generally speaking, pro-national and governmental-
activist factions will probably gain strength, in both parties.

(Text continued on page 107)

CHART III

ALLEGED EFFECTS OF APPORTIONMENT

Column headers (states, left to right):
ALABAMA, ALASKA, ARIZONA, ARKANSAS, CALIFORNIA, COLORADO, CONNECTICUT, DELAWARE, FLORIDA, GEORGIA, HAWAII, IDAHO, ILLINOIS, INDIANA, IOWA, KANSAS, KENTUCKY, LOUISIANA, MAINE, MARYLAND, MASSACHUSETTS, MICHIGAN, MINNESOTA[a], MISSISSIPPI, MISSOURI, MONTANA, NEBRASKA, NEVADA, NEW HAMPSHIRE, NEW JERSEY, NEW MEXICO, NEW YORK, NORTH CAROLINA, NORTH DAKOTA, OHIO, OKLAHOMA, OREGON, PENNSYLVANIA, RHODE ISLAND, SOUTH CAROLINA, SOUTH DAKOTA, TENNESSEE, TEXAS, UTAH, VERMONT, VIRGINIA, WASHINGTON, WEST VIRGINIA, WISCONSIN, WYOMING

I. ON PARTY[b]
- A. NONE
- B. PRO - DEMOCRATS
- C. PRO - REPUBLICANS
- D. PRO - DEMOCRATS AND REPUBLICANS
- E. OTHER

II. ON RACIAL DISCRIMINATION
- A. NONE[c]
- B. PRO - NEGROES
- C. PRO - WHITES

III. ON CITIES
- A. GENERAL ALLEGED EFFECTS[b]
  1. NONE
  2. PRO - RURAL (OVER - REPRESENTED)
  3. PRO - URBAN (OVER - REPRESENTED)
  4. PRO SOME CITIES, NOT OTHERS
  5. ANTI - SUBURBS, ESPECIALLY
  6. VARIES
- B. SPECIFIC ALLEGED EFFECTS[d]
  1. ON SHARING CERTAIN TAXES
  2. ON HIGHWAY AND BRIDGE BUILDING
  3. ON PUBLIC SCHOOL FINANCE
  4. ON BROADENING THE MUNICIPAL TAX BASE
  5. ON GENERAL OBSTACLE TO CITY PROGRAMS[e]
  6. ON OTHER
  7. NO COMPLAINTS OF ACTUAL DAMAGE

V. OTHER ELEMENTS
- A. PRESERVES HIGHER CULTURE
- B. RELIGIOUS DISCRIMINATION

CATEGORY FOOTNOTES FOR CHART III
"Alleged Effects of Apportionment"

a. The major portion of the data is based upon reports in William J. D. Boyd (ed.), *Compendium on Legislative Apportionment* (New York: National Municipal League, 1962). This list of alleged effects mainly concerns itself with *State* apportionment systems, although the effects of *congressional* apportionment are mentioned where appropriate.

b. Data are based upon the answers of the following questions for each State in *ibid.:* Do the inequities have the effect of discriminating against: (a) Either national party? (b) Rural or urban populations? (c) Any other elements?

c. An absence of racial discrimination as a result of apportionment was assumed if it was not specifically noted.

d. Data are based upon reports in *ibid.,* especially references to the following category: "complaints of actual damage attributable to discrimination."

e. E.g., welfare measures, home rule, zoning and planning, and urban renewal.

EXPLANATORY FOOTNOTES
"Alleged Effects of Apportionment"

1. Congressional districts.

2. Discrimination is alleged against one of the national parties, but neither is specified. (Max Yost, "Idaho," *Compendium,* op. cit., 27.)

3. *Congressional* apportionment does not appear to discriminate against either party. *State* legislative apportionment is alleged to discriminate against Republicans. Since both parties have both urban and rural sources of strength, neither is reported as being directly handicapped by an apportionment system favoring rural areas. Discrimination against urban districts is alleged to hurt the Republicans "only because much of the potential Republican vote lies in those areas." (Malcolm M. Jewell, "Kentucky," *ibid.,* 2.)

4. Nebraska elects its representatives to the unicameral legislature on a nonpartisan basis.

5. State Senate and House districts.

6. In the State Senate, "downstate" (Republican) areas are alleged to be favored.

7. The inequities are "so extreme in some cases" that they "cause many potential voters to look upon voting as futile. . . . I personally do not believe there is any deliberate attempt to discriminate against the Democratic party." (James S. Roberts, "Nevada," *ibid.,* 1.)

8. "Whatever partisan advantage either party may enjoy would appear to result largely from gerrymandering rather than from population disparities." (Ruth C. Silva, "New York," *ibid.*, 2.)

9. The current system favors the Republican outstate regions, especially in the State Senate and in Congress, "yet paradoxically the Republicans are also discriminated against by the general ticket aspects of the multi-member district set-up within Wayne County. . . ." (Charles W. Shull, "Michigan, *ibid.*, 2.)

10. The old apportionment of the legislature is alleged to have discriminated somewhat against the Democrats in the Senate and against the Republicans in the lower house.

11. "In the manner of districting, it is apparent that the personal interests of incumbent senators and representatives are a weighty consideration and the incumbents make common cause regardless of political party or rural-urban considerations when it comes to upsetting the present districting." (Mitchell J. Hunt, "Pennsylvania," *ibid.*, 2.)

12. Inequities in the size of senatorial districts affect the internal organization of the Democratic party since each senatorial district is represented by a man and woman on the State executive committee. Thus the urban populations are underrepresented in party affairs.

13. In the constitutional apportionment of 1901, the black-belt counties were given favorable treatment. Since then, they have opposed any reapportionment which would have threatened their control of the legislature. The growing power of the Negro vote may present Alabama legislators with the choice of either limiting black-belt influence or allowing for the possibility of the election of a Negro State Representative or Senator.

14. "Negro and oriental minorities, though not directly discriminated against through apportionment, are hurt by the discrimination against the urban areas in which they live." (James S. Roberts, "Nevada," *ibid.*, 2.)

15. Because of non-voting by Negroes and because in some communities the Negro vote is a controlled vote, the use of total population as a basis for representation may tend to give white voters in so-called "black belts" a disproportionate voice in the State legislature.

16. If, as a recently approved constitutional amendment provides, the vote is countywide for more than one Senator, the Negro bloc will be diluted in the general countywide tally. However, if State Senators are elected only by voters in their respective district, as a State court has ruled, those districts with a heavy Negro vote will be able to elect Negro Senators.

17. Democrats, in a suit filed in federal court, charged the Republican-controlled State government of deliberately discriminating against Negroes and Puerto Ricans in laying out the new lines for the 17th, 18th, 19th and

20th congressional districts in Manhattan. The suit, seeking to redraw the district boundaries, was dismissed. Representative Adam Clayton Powell, Jr., and other Harlem Democratic leaders opposed the suit and held that further reshaping of the four districts would deprive Negroes and Puerto Ricans of public offices they presently held.

18. Specific groups within the urban population are alleged to benefit from a system of apportionment weighted in behalf of rural areas: the banks, privately-owned utility companies, and insurance companies. (Paul Kelso, "Arizona," *ibid.*, 2.)

19. The upper house (Senate) is rurally dominated and has a majority from northern California.

20. "Voting in the legislature is most likely to follow a fractional and/or party line, when there is any pattern at all, rather than an urban-rural line." (Jewell, *loc. cit.*)

21. "There is little or no evidence of a rural conspiracy to deprive urbanites of representation." (Duane W. Hill, "Montana," *ibid.*, 2.)

22. "The present senatorial districts favor the 43 counties outside of the State's seven standard metropolitan areas." (Silva, *loc cit.*)

23. Reapportionment problems in North Carolina reflect a conflict between major geographical regions rather than urban-rural differences.

24. "Even with fair reapportionment, rural areas would dominate, but not to such a great extent." (Henry J. Tomasek, "North Dakota," *ibid.*, 2.)

24a. A suit was filed in the federal district court to have recent reapportionment bills invalidated. Governor Harrison called the April 1962 reapportionment fair "unless equality of population be permitted to overbalance completely all considerations of compactness, contiguity, habit, convenience of the people and community of interest." (*National Civic Review,* June 1962, 319.)

25. The lower house is heavily balanced in favor of Southern California and has more urban representation.

26. Republican party leaders in Oregon want more seats for rural areas, claiming city domination. The State's predominantly rural eastern plateau is seen as having been underrepresented in the legislature. *(New York Times,* August 19, 1962, 48.)

Proposed apportionment changes "would provide less representative government than that presently used." By the population standard of measurement "Oregon is the most equitably apportioned State in the Union." (*National Civic Review,* September 1962, 447.)

27. "Communities with large numbers of Armed Forces personnel are usually not given full credit for their populations." (Edward Lane-Reticker and James H. Ellis, "Connecticut," *Compendium, op cit.*, 2.)

28. "The most under-represented districts are neither urban nor rural, but suburban, and in the aggregate, suburban districts tend to be under-represented." (*Ibid.*)

29. Economic cleavages are mentioned as an important factor in legislative apportionment to be considered along with urban vs. rural interests.

"The problem of legislative apportionment in Arizona is further complicated by the position of Maricopa County as the center of population and the longstanding rivalry or conflict between Maricopa and Pima Counties." (Kelso, *op. cit.*, 3.)

30. "Unequally populated *Assembly* districts arise out of two situations: (1) State constitutional provisions which prevent crossing of county lines in forming an Assembly district; (2) Political gerrymandering. Since *Congressional* districts, according to the Constitution, must be composed of *contiguous* and *whole* Assembly districts, both constitutional provisions and gerrymandering lead to maldistricting in this case also. Unequal *Senate* districts, on the other hand, arise out of constitutional provisions established in the 1920's which set a maximum of one senator from each county, regardless of population." (Eugene C. Lee, "California," *ibid.*, 1.)

31. There is alleged heavy overrepresentation of rural areas in the State Senate. The urban congressional districts are overrepresented.

32. "The present *Congressional* districting law does not discriminate consistently against either urban or rural areas." (Silva, *loc. cit.*)

33. Rhode Island's two congressional districts do not discriminate against either rural or urban areas. In the legislature, urban areas are under-represented, especially in the State Senate.

34. "It is difficult to find specific examples of damage to urban interests resulting from under-representation." (Jewell, *op. cit.*, 3.)

35. The rural areas get a disproportionately high share of the gambling tax.

36. "Concrete consequences illustrating discrimination against cities are few; these few, difficult to prove or demonstrate." (Henry M. Alexander, "Arkansas," *ibid.*, 2.)

37. "There seems to be no evidence to indicate that the inequities of representation are in effect damaging." (John O. Stitely, "Rhode Island," *ibid.*, 2.)

38. Sectional differences are more important than urban-rural conflicts. Assembly welfare measures are often defeated in the Senate.

39. "Empirical studies have failed to reveal much of a (urban-rural) conflict in the legislative roll calls. Also, most of the troubles suffered by the metropolitan legislative programs and needs in the State legislature commonly are traceable to the cities' own delegates (and lack of inner unity

among them) rather than from any cohesive anti-urban outstate combine,"
nevertheless, the press blames urban underrepresentation as a major source
of metropolitan legislative troubles. (Robert F. Karsch, "Missouri," *ibid.*, 2.)

40. "Despite the interest of both houses in rural issues, urban issues
frequently receive more favorable reaction and higher priority than they
would in a good many other States." (Duane W. Hill, "Montana," *ibid.*, 3.)

41. "It is difficult to attribute such 'damage' to the mere matter of
apportionment." (Hunt, *op. cit.*, 2.)

42. Against "liberals."

43. Labor elements are alleged to be discriminated against. (Manning J.
Dauer, "Florida," *ibid.*)

44. South Mississippians claim the coastal industries in their area do not
receive sufficient attention due to underrepresentation.

45. "There is certainly *mathematical inequity*, with discrimination in favor
of the rural and against the urban population. There appear to be *very few
indications of legislation where rural and urban representatives* in the General Assembly *divided clearly.*" (David Welborn, "Indiana," *ibid.*, 1.)

46. "Through talks with Nebraska legislators, one is convinced . . . that
there has been no rural conspiracy to deprive the urban population of
equitable representation." (A. B. Winter, "Nebraska," *ibid.*, 1.)

47. The black-belt counties which control the legislature "historically
have been the cultural and educational centers of the State and have provided it with its most able political leadership." (James E. Larson, "Alabama," *ibid.*, 2.)

48. Northern Louisiana which is rural and heavily Protestant (and has
a high percentage of Negro population) is alleged to benefit from a malapportionment which discriminates against the large urban Catholic population in the southern part of the State. However, "the damage attributable
to this inequity is not readily discernible." (William C. Havard, "Louisiana,"
ibid., 1.)

Finally the internal government of parties would be affected by
changes in apportionment in some States. Georgia and Texas are
prominent examples.[3] In many other States, local party delegations
to State conventions are based on existing legislative districts.

---

[3] Cf. Sanders v. Gray, F. Supp. 158 (N. D. Ga., 1962), *appeal docketed,*
No. 959, 370 U.S. 921 (1962) where the county unit system of weighting
votes for nominations to State office was nullified.

The Roles of Legislators

The detailed impact on leadership and governance that changes would bring is difficult to forecast. It relates to the relations between representatives and constituents. The legislature is a complicated body.[4] Its members are numerous and often specialized in the legislative tasks they perform. Each member is likely to have several different roles to play, all of which are ultimately synthesized. In considering changes in apportionment, we cannot believe that new warm machines are to be substituted for old warm machines, with slightly different instructions wired in because of a balancing of district populations or a straightening of district lines. The whole possible range of effects has to be scrutinized.

The roles and tasks of the legislators can be partially known by the sources of the bills that they consider. In Table II, are listed the sources of bills before the 1941 New York State Legislature, as revealed by painstaking study.

From the table, we surmise that the legislator must devote himself to a stream of communications coming from many executive and judicial agencies and from many districts not his own. The extent to which his own district is affected by the legislative work will vary from term to term, but will never be more than a small fraction of the whole. The executive is a more fecund source of laws than the legislature itself. Pressure groups are important. So are government employees. Bills coming from private individuals are few in number and if these few be examined there can be little doubt that their sponsors are mostly "big shots," that is people of some power, position, and connections. Where are the people who are being "unequally represented"? The answer is plain—in the same place where the people who would be "equally represented" are: nowhere and everywhere.

---

[4] Gosnell, *op. cit.*, chaps. VIII-XII. The studies of Professor Warren Miller of the Survey Research Center, University of Michigan, promise to be the best thus far on the representative-constituent relation. The writings of T. V. Smith should not be neglected (*The Legislative Way of Life,* 1940), nor of Lewis A. Dexter ("The Representative and His District," 16 *Human Organization,* no. 1, p. 2).

TABLE II. SOURCES OF BILLS
Before the Legislature of New York State, 1941 [1]

Sources	Number of Proposals Introduced	Number of Proposals Enacted
Administrative		
Federal agencies	14	4
State departments	376	240
Independent commissions	8	6
Local government agencies	348	241
State and local officials	23	11
Total	769	502
Judicial		
Court and court officials	56	28
State judicial council	32	19
Total	88	47
Legislative		
Law revision commission	51	44
Temporary legislative committees and commissioners	87	47
Legislators	31	28
Total	169	119
Governmental employee associations	97	28
Non-governmental		
Organizations	395	110
Individuals or unorganized groups	123	78
Total	518	188
Total of proposals on which information is available	1,641	884
Proposals on which source information is lacking	1,199	71
GRAND TOTAL	2,840	955

[1] Elizabeth McK. Scott and Belle Zeller, "State Agencies and Law-making," 2 *Public Administration Review* (1942), 205-220.

Changes would occur but they would have nothing to do with "equal representation." If the legislative apportionment is fixed to reflect the same sources as the Governor's authority, I should estimate that three effects might be expected to occur: the amount of servicing of the district ("nursing the constituency," the British say) will increase; the executive branch's desires will be more automatically and completely correlated with legislative activity; the prestige of legislators will decline somewhat. If the Governor is charged with reapportionment, the same phenomena will be reinforced.

A more direct study of how legislators spend their time is afforded by the Wahlke, Eulau, Buchanan, and Ferguson study of the 474 members of the California, New Jersey, Ohio, and Tennessee legislatures.[5] The legislator is, to varying degrees, an expert on one or more of the dozen major categories of concerns of the legislatures. Fifty-one members of the four legislatures were singled out as persons on whom one relied upon for expert advice and directions on these concerns; they received 55 percent of all nominations made by all legislators as to who the experts were. Reapportionment probably reduces the expertness of the legislature as a whole; compensatory advantages must therefore be sought.

A second set of roles of the legislator are called by the same scholars "purposive roles." These include the "ritualist" who devotes himself to mastering and carrying on the complicated routines of the house; the "tribune" who acts as advocate and defender of the people; the "inventor" who devises methods of handling legislation and organizes ideas; and the "broker" who appeases and coordinates conflicting and uncomprehending views of issues. In Ohio, for example, 67 percent of the members appear upon interview to see themselves as "ritualists," 40 percent as "tribunes," 33 percent as "inventors" and 48 percent as "brokers." (A number see themselves as holding double or even triple roles.)

On top of the purposive roles come the "representative roles." A

---

[5] John A. Wahlke, Heinz Eulau, William Buchanan, and Leroy C. Ferguson, *The Legislative System* (New York: Wiley, 1962). Cf. Havard and Beth, *op. cit.,* 110.

legislator may have a "trustee" orientation, viewing himself as an agent free to follow his knowledge and conscience. His orientation may be that of "delegate," wherein he seeks to determine and follow the wishes of his constituents. Or he may be the "politico" who moves back and forth, not always logically, between the other two orientations. In California, for instance, 55 percent of the members are placed in the category of "trustee," 25 percent into that of "politico," and 20 percent into the role of "delegate." Less than 20 percent of all four houses see carrying out the wishes of their constituents as an important definition of their mission. This finding would seem to make the theories of "equal-populations" advocates rather far-fetched and academic. Can anyone reasonably believe, in the face of such evidence, that "equal representation" has a practical meaning that is true to the vision of equality?

Third, the legislators have different conceptions of their constituency, some confining it narrowly to their electoral district, others to the broader reaches of the State and still others to both at various times. The "areal" role, the authors call it. More Tennessee legislators seem to be district-oriented than legislators from the other States studied. Perhaps about a fourth of all the legislators are state-oriented, a little more are of mixed orientation and about half are district-oriented.

Table III indicates that a sense of the whole-state interest is found more among delegates from less-populated areas. The metropolitan representatives view their tasks more as servicing their individual districts. This effect would possibly be amplified under reapportionment along equal-populations lines. That is, orientations towards narrow district interests might increase. This is a reason why, although increased seats in metropolitan centers may appear better for the greater part of the people, they might not *work* better: the great problem in American representation is *community* representation, not *equal-populations districts.* If a set of city blocks in Detroit gets two seats where it had one before, the extra representative will more than likely be a constituent-service type, not a type who will help bring into focus the total vision of the Detroit metropolitan area as a *community.*

111

TABLE III

Relation Between Electoral Competition,
Sense of Mission, and Location of District

Degree of Attention and Orientation of Individual Legislators	Metropolitan			Over 50% Urban		
	Compet-itive (N=48) %	Semi-Comp. (N=38) %	One-Party (N=39) %	Compet-itive (N=20) %	Semi-Comp. (N=35) %	One Party (N=50) %
1) Largely District	52	47	31	60	46	30
2) Largely District-State	24	32	28	30	40	42
3) Largely State	24	21	41	10	14	28

Note: The table shows results from three States, California, New Jersey, and Ohio. Complex definitions were employed for "competitive," etc., but generally, "competitive" meant "un-safe" seats.

Source: With minor verbal adaptations, from John C. Wahlke, Heinz Eulau, William Buchanan, and Leroy C. Ferguson, *The Legislative System* (New York: Wiley, 1962), 293.

Racial Discrimination in Apportionment

On the question of racial discrimination, it would appear that State apportionments are uniformly free from bias. That is not to say that no effects on the political power of racially organized groupings exist. Detroit has more Negroes than the Upper Peninsula; ergo, if Negro rights required equal-populations districts, Negroes would be discriminated against. There have been voiced some opinions of this kind. For instance, Justice Douglas stated in *South* v. *Peters,*[6] that urban centers were the only places where Negroes voted in important numbers in the South and they were therefore heavily disenfranchised by the county unit system method

---

[6] 339 U. S. 276 (1950).

of election in the political parties of Georgia. But, by the same token, the potential advantage lying with the large numbers of Negroes in the rural "black-belt" counties is great, once they achieve the vote. A bird in the hand may be worth two in the bush, but the hand should not be holding this bird.

Thus in Alabama, our informant tells us, the counties of responsible leadership, higher culture, and large proportion of Negroes are favored in the present apportionment system. And in Louisiana, the Catholics of the densely populated South, again indirectly, are presumed to be discriminated against by the apportionment system that favors the Northern Protestant parishes. And the Chairman of the Executive Board of the American Jewish Committee, Mr. M. B. Abram, speaking before the group, has said that reapportionment is linked to the increasing political power of important "religious and ethnic minorities in this country." [7] Mr. Abram, who as attorney argued against the Georgia apportionment system before the U. S. District Court in Atlanta and who as member of the Board of Trustees of the Twentieth Century Fund helped to sponsor a conference and report on behalf of reapportionment of the States, has been a staunch advocate of the abstract principle of "one man—one vote."

The pressure of demographic effects in apportionment schemes is used by the advocates of equal-populations districts both to condemn the existing system and to praise the new. If one so-called minority is holding up the majority's program, why do equal-populations advocates justify a new scheme on behalf of new minorities? They should be explicit so that a court of law and of opinion can judge whether they are truly majority advocates or minority advocates. I guess that a psychological principle, not a logical one, explains their contradiction: They have majoritarian complexes in minority bosoms.

But again ethnic and religious effects, if they exist, are indirectly produced by the way the population groups itself. If Jews and Catholics, Poles or Canadians, move into suburbs, they often fall into heavily-peopled districts. If Catholic French-Canadians move

---

[7] *The New York Times,* November 12, 1962.

into rural districts of Maine, they will be overrepresented. The demographic picture changes constantly. If Negroes move into the centers of cities, they fall into lightly-peopled districts and are "over-represented" in Mr. Abram's terms, as is the case with Congressman William Dawson's district in Chicago. It is just another indication of the quality of statistical reasoning used by Mr. Abram and many another that the difference between the population of Congressman Dawson's Negro district in Chicago and the nearby Caucasian Republican 4th district is greater than the total of all Negroes voting in several Southern States in 1960—119,300.

It may be wondered whether the confusion of population change is not in itself an argument for equal-populations districts. But the confusion is natural to all historical situations, and that something must be done for the sake of doing something is highly questionable. Furthermore, if something is to be done, whoever does it will be deeply immersed in political discriminations, without end. More-over, the equal-populations principle creates as many (or more, in my opinion) problems as it solves. And then the effects are not at all clear, even from the standpoint of the ethnic group concerned. Therefore, to intervene in apportionment to prevent accidental or indirect ethnic favoritism may be unwise, especially if done by an unwieldy and inconstant judicial process.

Effects on City and Country

Would not the question of urban discrimination be more revealing of the effects of apportionments? There, at least, as Chart III shows, 45 States are alleged to favor rural elements. The formal causes here are in large measure the attempt to grant communities definite representation and the failure to reapportion over time. The specific effects of the favoring of less urban areas are not so confidently expressed by informed observers, as the Chart shows. In 23 States, no allegation of actual damage owing to anti-urban discrimination is made. It will be noted too that the specific complaints are in vast majority matters of finances. In over 20 States, rural or less urban areas are said to get more than their share of taxes; in eight States, more than their share of highway and bridge construction; in six more than their share of public school monies.

If a *prima facie* case can be made for the cities here, it can be made for the less populated areas too. Very generally stated, one widely held doctrine of taxation and spending is the progressive principle: taxing is according to ability to pay, spending is according to need. Probably most advocates of wholesale reapportionment would approve these principles. The apportionment system therefore may be assuring the poorer areas of many States that those who need, get—in roads, schools, and services; it may even occur that the city representatives contribute willingly in many cases to this disproportion of spending, just as, for example, the Congressmen from large Eastern cities will tax their own constituents disproportionately heavily in order to give disproportionately large benefits to Wyoming, Arkansas, Mississippi, and Alabama.

The mayor of Nashville, Tennessee, a plaintiff in the case of *Baker* v. *Carr*, caused to be prepared an elaborate book of 73 large pages crammed with facts—but not all the facts. Charts were prepared showing that "underrepresented" counties had less than their "equal quota" of State aid to education (see Figure 7) and State gasoline tax receipts (see Figure 8). No mention was made of the progressive principle of government spending. Yet when new economic information is supplied in the form of the percent of families in each county who earned less than $3,000 a year (see the upper scale imposed on Figure 7), a likely substitute rationale is immediately indicated. The legislature is not "discriminating against the populous counties." It is helping the poorer counties to educate their children and pay their costs of government.[8] (Note the same phenomenon in Figure 8).[9] Since in most States of the country, the resources of the rural areas are less than those of the cities, a certain measure of difference in spending patterns in favor of the rural

---

[8] This is apart from the question whether the smaller the school district the higher the per pupil expenditure should be, which is yet another principle arbitrating against the "discrimination" theory.

[9] This is apart from the additional question whether road networks in rural areas require more spending per capita.

Figure 7

IMPOSITION OF A POOR-RICH SCALE TO EXPLAIN THE SEEMING
DISCRIMINATION AGAINST "UNDER-REPRESENTED" COUNTIES
COMPARISION OF THE 1959-60 STATE AID TO EDUCATION FOR COUNTIES
OVER AND UNDER REPRESENTED BY DIRECT REPRESENTATIVES IN
THE 1961 TENNESSEE STATE HOUSE OF REPRESENTATIVES*

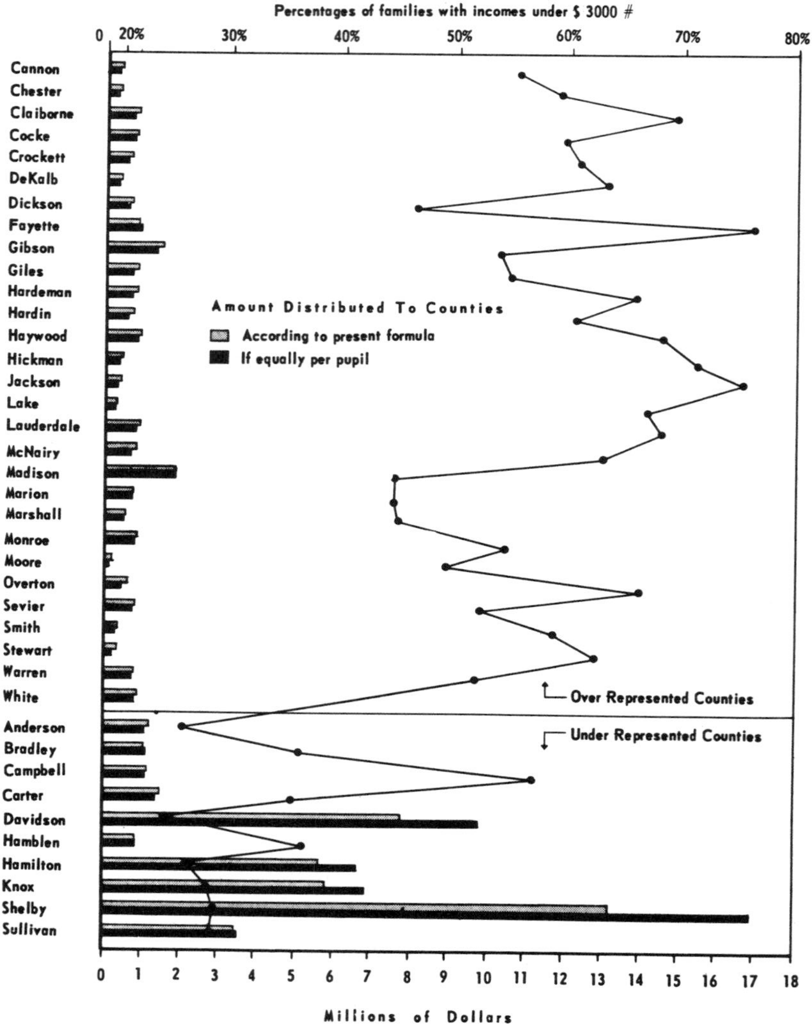

* CITY OF NASHVILLE, <u>LEGISLATIVE APPORTIONMENT IN TENNESSEE</u>,CENTRAL PRINTING OFFICE, NASHVILLE, 1961, Chart -5

\# U.S. BUREAU OF CENSUS, COUNTY AND CITY DATA BOOK, U.S. GOVERNMENT PRINTING OFFICE, WASHINGTON, D.C., 1962, Table 2, Tennessee

116

Figure 8

IMPOSITION OF A POOR-RICH SCALE TO EXPLAIN THE SEEMING
DISCRIMINATION AGAINST "UNDER-REPRESENTED" COUNTIES
COMPARISION OF THE 1959-60 TWO CENT GASOLINE TAX DISTRIBUTION FOR
COUNTIES OVER AND UNDER REPRESENTED BY DIRECT REPRESENTATIVES
IN THE 1961 TENNESSEE STATE HOUSE OF REPRESENTATIVES*

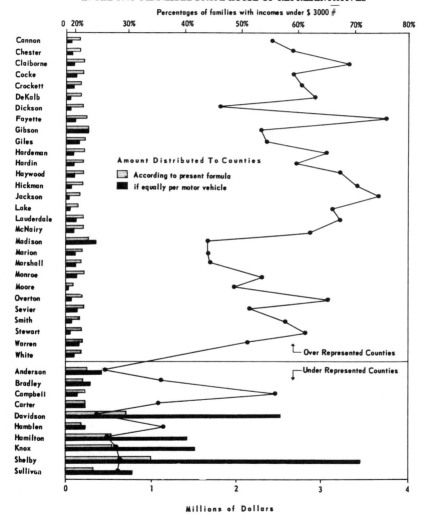

*CITY OF NASHVILLE, <u>LEGISLATIVE APPORTIONMENT IN TENNESSEE</u>,CENTRAL PRINTING OFFICE, NASHVILLE, 1961, Chart-5
U.S. BUREAU OF CENSUS, COUNTY AND CITY DATA BOOK. U.S. GOVERNMENT PRINTING OFFICE, WASHINGTON, D.C., 1962, Table 2, Tennessee

areas is to be expected in most States and is fully in keeping with the theories of spending cherished by the liberal advocates of the equal-populations principle. One could argue a strong case, using many examples from the agrarian discontent of other countries and other times, as well as from American history, that an erasing of small community "overrepresentation" would result in the degradation and impoverishment of non-metropolitan America.

The flow of funds into and out of the treasury of a State is bewildering; locating the headwaters and plotting the delta streams are tasks for large computers programmed by genuises. There is little possibility of and less reason to connect them directly with the details of apportionment. To say, for example, that because apportionment is not perfectly modalized with population, New York City gets so many dollars less per capita per pupil, or so many dollars less for public works [10] is not only quite unproven and unlikely to be proved, but the assertion itself implies that the reason for seeking more power at the capital is to change the flow of dollars, offices, and favors to the new powerholders. It is an implied threat to gang up on behalf of new local interests. Should the day come when these objectives are attained, no doubt they will have to be accepted and perhaps they may be on balance *pro bono publico*. But to ask for sheer power politics to be carried to fulfillment under the auspices of "equal protection of the laws" is presumptuous.

---

[10] WMCA v. Simon, brief of plaintiffs. Actually, with 46% of the population in 1960, New York City received 53% of general per capita State aid in 1962-63, and lesser or greater proportions of various other aid programs. Since over 50 different formulas are used to determine shares of various programs, it is clear that many values are involved; to insist upon judging this complex picture on sheer population grounds, and especially when only convenient to do so, is absurd and unjust. Cf. R. M. Haig and Carl S. Shoup, *The Financial Problem of the City of New York* (Albany, 1952), 359-60. The same authors conclude that the "data do not indicate that New York City is a victim of discrimination in the distribution of state grants." (363) New York City's figures indicate a 50.7% increase in State aid receipts in 1962-3 when compared with 1958-9 (last fiscal year of the preceding administration); this and other data are grounds for believing that the situation might permit arguing the other way, if advocates of other parts of the State wished to do so.

The Great Lakes-St. Lawrence Waterway issue, which endured in an active form for half a century and will last much longer, pitted a number of interests of Upstate New York against various interests of New York City. Most informed Americans are probably pleased with the way in which the Seaway developed and probably most New Yorkers as well. Yet "New York City"—that is, the New York City legislators—fought the upstate cities for many years to block the Seaway. Would the Seaway be there now if the present apportionment plan had not existed? A flat "No!" to this question is not possible. People have a way of working around all sorts of obstacles when they are determined and are given a chance. But perhaps the apportionment plan was implicitly intended to help out upstate interests (and indirectly the interests of the whole) in precisely such circumstances as the Great Lakes-St. Lawrence Seaway development.

Some 15 State legislatures are said to present general obstacles to city programs as a result of their apportionment systems (see Chart III). These have to do with home-rule authority, urban renewal, welfare, etc. Parts of the allegations are undoubtedly correct; it would be astonishing if ever a lower-level government did not find its programs—even highly desirable ones—sometimes blocked by a higher-level authority. It must be realized, however, that (a) these programs are not unanimously regarded with favor within the cities; (b) some cities sometimes oppose the favorite programs of other cities; (c) the cities of America are not known for the great vision of their plans nor for their selfless enthusiasm where local politics do not benefit from a plan to glorify the whole city.

A constant problem with reapportionment advocates is their simplism. They speak of city against country, or urban against rural, but in an increasing number of States the rural population is dwindling. If there is a demographic conflict (and why shouldn't there be?), it is between upstate-downstate city interests (as, Buffalo vs. New York City), or small city vs. large city (as Peoria vs. Chicago).[11] Most important of all is the development of suburbs, which turn out to contain the districts most unequal in population

---

[11] Cf. footnotes 20, 21, 38, and 40 on Chart III.

size on the "underrepresented" side. In New York City, Chicago, and elsewhere, the central city population has achieved lately a point of relative decline. As Gordon Baker has pointed out "if the city can manage to lose enough people, it may, ironically, eventually attain its equal share of legislative representation." [12] In that case, we shall all be happy because, by the logic of the equal-populations advocates, New York City will suddenly and whilst we sleep become a marvel of good government.

In 1961 the so-called Bowman Bill was introduced into the Michigan legislature. This bill prohibited the City of Detroit from levying an income tax on persons working in Detroit and resident outside the city. The suburban legislators, regardless of party, supported the bill and the legislators from Detroit opposed it en bloc. The bill passed and was vetoed by the Governor. That the veto may have been an important factor in the Governor's defeat at the polls in 1962 is indicated by his losses in ordinarily Democratic suburbs. On an issue such as this, the system of apportionment counts, but equal-populations districts might only have reinforced the victory of the anti-tax forces.

The suburbs thus do not necessarily share the interests of their neighboring cities. They may be resisting highways, blocking industry, opposing planning, and fighting consolidation. Are these actions good or bad? If bad, and most planners and National Municipal League members would say they are bad, then why reinforce them by reapportioning the State? For the sake of an unnecessary abstract dogma of equal numbers? Another group supporting reapportionment has been some labor unions, such as the ILGWU, in New York; are they fully aware now that New York City, especially Manhattan Borough, will not gain relatively as many seats as the suburban counties will in any equal-populations districting? No doubt there is an inertia among reapportionment advocates. They have been "fighting the good fight" so long that it is painful to desist, even if their opponents will gain the fruits of victory.

---

[12] *Op. cit.,* 57.

It is sometimes implied that the quality of representation is a function of the size of the district. Actually, this argument is implied rather than made explicit because of the obvious contradictions to it. For instance, the average quality of representatives in the U. S. Senate, which is the most extremely biased of all American apportionments against the equal-populations principle, is generally reputed to be superior to the average of the House of Representatives. Within the House itself, to take an instance, Sam Rayburn came from a district of small population in Texas, Albert Thomas from one of the largest. Would the advocates of "equal representation" wish to equalize these two men? Many other instances might be adduced where it is obvious that disproportions of population are not producing less favorable results than could otherwise be expected, from the viewpoint of the State or the nation. Those who talk of the need for a shift of seats must ultimately rest their case for the *quality* of representation on bread-and-butter grounds. They feel that statistically the shift will bring, not a greater number of qualified men, or men with a State-wide or nation-wide viewpoint, but men who would tend to the local needs of the newly created suburban districts or growing city districts. I have already indicated that not only may a deterioration in the quality of representatives occur, but that the major problems of metropolitan America will probably not be assisted towards a solution by the change.

Table IV is a crude attempt to present, in the absence of other evidence, a comparison of certain activities of two groups of cities, to see whether the cities of States with districts generally very unbalanced in population fare differently than those of States where equal-populations districts are more common. A comparison is suggested by such facts as that Georgia's often-abused county unit apportionment has not kept Atlanta from being one of the best-governed cities of America. The top-ten and the bottom-ten of Professors David and Eisenberg's list of States ranked on the "index of representativeness" (it is of course really an index of "equipopulationism") of their legislatures are presented along with per capita budget items. The averages indicate that it would be difficult to distinguish the two groups without the "index." That is, if unequal

121

Table IV. Top Ten States of Unequalized Population in Districts (*)
Per Capita Spending on Selected Indices of Welfare of Largest City in Each

State	General Revenue (1)	Taxes (2)	Intergovernmental Revenue (3)	General Expenditure (all functions capital outlay) (4)	Police Protection (5)	Fire (6)	Highways (total) (7)	Sewerage (total) (8)	Parks & Recreation (9)	Health & Hospitals (10)	Education (11)	Public Welfare (12)	Housing & Urban Renewal (13)	Total Debt (14)	No. of professional planning employees per 10,000 pop. (15)
Florida (Miami)	112.15	86.89	2.70	88.15	19.65	16.92	7.53	8.88	9.96	.47	—	—	.15	298.86	0
Nevada (Las Vegas)	96.34	64.98	4.89	71.14	19.14	12.92	9.72	3.28	7.24	.53	—	—	—	58.96	4
Delaware (Wilmington)	181.46	86.52	61.82	156.92	14.73	13.47	18.02	4.60	10.60	1.64	96.57	.28	—	429.98	0
Maryland (Baltimore)	248.71	124.23	101.63	197.31	23.15	15.07	31.69	4.83	8.12	14.98	77.60	26.86	20.02	372.71	12
Connecticut (Hartford)	222.69	168.72	30.87	177.88	16.29	19.03	10.65	—	13.05	15.85	71.03	12.62	12.98	174.73	6
Rhode Island (Providence)	192.69	121.14	41.03	155.56	16.47	13.43	11.16	6.36	6.54	9.43	62.34	10.70	19.61	340.31	16
Ohio (Cleveland)	97.21	58.21	17.83	74.64	18.12	10.67	12.02	6.99	8.66	2.78	—	1.26	11.22	305.13	15
Georgia (Atlanta)	77.45	44.51	5.93	57.24	10.99	9.05	15.63	9.84	4.85	.74	.07	.07	.57	232.60	14
Alabama (Birmingham)	63.70	32.18	11.36	47.66	9.29	9.85	3.76	5.54	1.38	2.93	—	.12	.45	281.76	7(**)
New Mexico (Albuquerque)	71.68	50.95	3.29	56.82	11.31	7.87	11.04	26.80	4.27	.89	—	—	—	270.23	6
Average	136.41	83.83	28.14	108.33	15.91	12.83	13.12	8.57	7.47	5.02	—	—	—	276.53	—

Per Capita Spending on Selected Indices of Welfare of Largest City in Each

States	General Revenue (1)	Taxes (2)	Intergovernmental Revenue (3)	General Expenditure (all functions capital outlay) (4)	Police Protection (5)	Fire (6)	Highways (total) (7)	Sewerage (total) (8)	Parks & Recreation (9)	Health & Hospitals (10)	Education (11)	Public Welfare (12)	Housing & Urban Renewal (13)	Total Debt (14)	No. of professional planning employees per 10,000 pop. (15)
Massachusetts (Boston)	320.09	216.84	86.83	283.52	27.06	18.56	10.25	2.20	7.68	30.39	56.36	60.72	.30	211.27	66
Virginia (Richmond)	196.71	124.54	46.99	180.09	15.02	12.08	12.97	7.69	6.63	3.19	75.66	31.23	9.81	398.50	6
Oregon (Portland)	88.68	53.15	8.06	72.05	17.17	15.68	9.27	6.43	15.71	2.53	—	—	—	107.44	19
Wisconsin (Milwaukee)	125.99	66.29	38.61	93.27	18.79	11.46	23.93	13.01	9.09	4.34	9.78	.01	1.24	237.69	23
West Virginia (Charleston)	24.42	48.20	.34	52.42	9.67	8.53	9.51	4.91	3.78	1.27	—	—	—	140.20	—
Arkansas (Little Rock)	57.56	24.12	10.56	46.01	9.77	8.88	11.73	3.88	3.60	1.90	—	—	—	150.33	2
Nebraska (Omaha)	64.51	44.11	7.40	45.52	9.55	8.49	15.37	31.36	3.99	1.45	—	—	—	68.81	4
Kentucky (Louisville)	118.51	57.46	12.87	86.71	9.62	6.89	5.49	17.42	4.85	6.99	24.07	2.30	15.89	377.53	8*
New Hampshire (Manchester)	118.65	102.03	8.20	107.93	7.59	10.92	21.24	.33	3.48	1.60	44.92	6.55	—	106.39	2
South Dakota (Sioux Falls)	75.98	50.27	6.63	42.77	6.92	7.03	11.01	11.61	21.74	1.04	—	.09	—	65.27	1
Average	119.11	78.70	22.64	101.03	13.12	10.85	13.08	9.88	8.06	5.47	—	—	—	186.34	—

(*) Selected from "Table 6—Per Capita Amounts of Selected Financial Items: 1961," from U. S. Department of Commerce, *Compendium of City Government Finances in 1961* (Washington: United States Government Printing, Office, 1962). Last column is number of professional planning employees per ten thousand population, derived from "Table 12, Planning Data for Cities over 10,000, 1962," Nolting, S., Orin, F., *et al.*, eds., *The Municipal Yearbook 1962* (Chicago: International City Managers' Association, 1962). It is of significance that only three of these States have legislative apportionments older than 1955 (Delaware 1897; Conn. S-1876 and H-1903; and R. I. H-1930 and S-1940).
(**) 1960 data.

or equal district populations make a difference in the ultimate financial and service picture of the largest cities, that difference is not evident in these general statistics of two extreme groups.[13] Nor is it likely, therefore, that the 30 States in between would show the sought-for differences. Of what value then are the lengthy lists of statistics on unequal districts if they do not correlate with anything? Their only function is to reflect by numbers magic the dogma on which they are based.

Professor Gordon E. Baker has treated directly of possible discrimination against cities in a work entitled *Rural Versus Urban Political Power*.[14] Some of the many activities of State legislatures concerning cities that he enumerates[15] appear *prima facie* to be uninformed and regrettable to this writer and, I am sure, to many others. Others appear desirable. As Professor Richard Snyder says in his introduction to the work, "Unfortunately, the matter is not simply one of amassing evidence of the blatant inequities in political representation, of the lack of correspondence between jurisdictional units on the one hand and revenue sources and needs on the other." Although Professor Baker's work contains more specific allegations of consequences than any other known to this writer, his conclusions were perforce general and taken "on faith." The consequences are not clearly shown to attend upon apportionment; the consequences are "good" for some, "bad" for others; and the consequences of reapportionment by equal population districts are not calculated. This faithful advocate of reapportionment concludes: "While equal representation is no panacea for all urban problems, it can at least clarify the question of responsibility and provide a sounder psychological climate for political institutions." My contention is the

---

[13] The sign test on the categories for which means are indicated in the table shows a merely chance difference among the categories: $- X^2 = .363 > 750\%$. Why haven't the Council of State Governments, the National Municipal League, and other interested groups gone into detailed statistical analysis along these lines? I have merely pointed the way here to what might be much more valid findings, if appropriate correlational techniques were applied.

[14] New York, 1955.

[15] Page 28 *et passim*.

contrary, and proposals to bring about "responsibility" and "a sounder psychological climate" are contained in the last chapter of this work.

A second, later study may be reported, that of Robert S. Friedman,[16] which analyzes a number of interviews of Tennessee legislators on issues involving urban-rural differences, and contains a general survey of the literature on the subject. Professor Friedman's conclusions deserve extensive quotation:

> Evidence elicited from an exploratory study of urban-rural conflict as perceived by a sample of Tennessee legislators leads to the conclusion that urbanness and ruralness are far less useful in explaining the political processes in the United States than more detailed interest groupings. This alone does not represent a startling revelation. What is important is that as readjustments in the social and economic structure of urban and rural areas continue to take place this will become more pronounced, perhaps to an extent that ultimately the terms urban and rural will cease to have any usefulness in differentiating political interests.
>
> However, notions about urban-rural conflicts have permeated the language of politics to such an extent that not only will terms like urban-rural conflict, urban-rural cleavage, and city slicker and country hick persist as part of the language, but by definition they will continue to be part of the process. They will remain important as part of the folklore, part of the technique of political struggle, and part of the ideology of the participants regardless of whether they represent competing forces in the process or not.[17]

Another pertinent study of the clash of metropolitan and non-metropolitan interests dealt with the State legislatures of Illinois and Missouri.[18] Its conclusions are of great importance to considerations of apportionment. In it, Professor Derge compares the voting be-

---

[16] "The Urban-Rural Conflict Revisited," *Western Political Quarterly*, June 1961, 481. This article does not appear to have found its way into into the voluminous judicial citations in Baker v. Carr. Cf. Howard W. Beers, "Rural-Urban Differences: Some Evidence from Public Opinion Polls," *Rural Sociology*, March 1953, 1.

[17] *Ibid.*, 495.

[18] David R. Derge, "Metropolitan and Outstate Alignments in Illinois and Missouri Legislative Delegations," *American Political Science Review*, December 1958, 1065. Cf. C. H. Hyneman, "The Indiana General Assembly," in *1958 Governor's Pre-Legislative Conference* (Bloomington, Ind.: Bureau of Government Research, 1958).

havior of metropolitan and non-metropolitan legislators. He reports that the non-metropolitan members seldom vote as a bloc against the metropolitan; nor do the metropolitan members usually vote together. When the city legislators *do* vote together they usually prevail. Unless proponents of general reapportionment can counter this finding to a significant degree, a major part of their case must crumble.

A second significant study, reported by Wheeler and Bebout, was completed by George D. Young and deals with the special session of the Missouri General Assembly in 1958, called to consider "emergency" legislation requested by the administrations of St. Louis and Kansas City.[19] Reports the author: "In the House the difficulty in passing city legislation does not come from rural members but from members of the city's own delegation. . . . It is almost invariably true that if the city's delegation is united upon a measure it will be accepted by the entire General Assembly." The legislation failed of passage! This evidence is damaging enough to the non-empirical and simplistic theory of the country as the source of the city's woes.[20] But in addition, Missouri happens to be one of the States most closely apportioned on an equal-populations basis. And in both houses!

Relation to the Majority Principle

The significance of apportionment systems to the majority principle takes several theoretical forms. To carry out "rationally" any single form usually invokes so many other factors that unforeseen effects occur. Apportionment can facilitate majority rather than minority government, and *vice versa*. It can foster one kind of majority over another. It can dampen either majority or minority rule by promoting compromise.[21]

---

[19] George D. Young, "The 1958 Special Session of the Missouri General Assembly," *Missouri Political Science Association Newsletter,* 3 (1958), quoted in John P. Wheeler and John E. Bebout, "After Reapportionment," *National Civic Review,* May 1962.

[20] Including the present author's overstatement of the inadequate evidence, in *Elements of Political Science, op. cit.*

[21] Cf. e.g., note 26, Chart III.

Apportionment can be used to accomplish majorities that come out of the whole population or the voting population (usually co-terminal) by being based upon some preferred type of whatever persistent attitudes and groupings are discoverable in the State. Thus, if one is willing to bank on the Democratic Party urban "liberal" position, he would probably prefer to reduce the population of central urban districts, thus increasing their number, and to draw their boundaries without regard to racial, economic, ethnic, or religious groupings. The majorities that ensue in the legislature may carry forward a more active, if perhaps more turbulent and kaleido-scopic, program. If a person dislikes the kind of government of cities and States that has come from either Party, he may wish to retain the present system or devise a new one.

It should be indicated here that majority rule does not need much encouragement. We are in an early stage of investigation of the subject, but there is some evidence that a so-called "cube law" of legislative seats holds for legislatures based on plurality-system elections. Under this "law," for every percentage point of increase over 50 percent of the popular vote in an election, the winning party wins a higher percentage of seats.[22] Thus, if a party wins 53 percent of the popular vote, it is likely to gain 59.2 percent of the seats. This hypothetical case can be matched by a number of actual American and British cases. The same strange mathematical phenomenon is sensed somewhat subsconsciously by advocates of the status quo in legislative apportionment. They feel that they may be letting in a tiger if they admit the kitten. It is the distribution of seats by the community principle that blocks the cube law of majorities from exhibiting a fuller impact. Whether the result is good or bad depends on one's philosophy or feelings, and upon a knowledge, unfortunately very scanty, of exactly what majorities and compromises would ensue.

---

[22] James G. March, "Party Legislative Representation as a Function of Election Results," *Public Opinion Quarterly* (Winter 1957-8), 521. The equation of the Cube Law reads

$$Y = \frac{3X^3}{3X^2 - 3X + 1}$$ where Y is the proportion of seats in an assembly and X is the proportion of votes.

The United States is increasingly urban. The apportionment arguments of 50 years ago are already somewhat archaic and irrelevant. For example, the New York State Constitution was challenged as causing through its apportionment provisions a minority rule by the rural areas of the State. Yet only 23 of 62 New York counties are below 40 percent urban. These 23 rural-urban counties have 23 assembly seats and 6 3/10 Senate seats. If New York City's State legislators combine with all other legislators from the New York Metropolitan region (i.e., with Nassau, Suffolk, Westchester, and Rockland Counties), they would carry a majority of the legislature (i.e., 81 of 150 Assembly seats and 30½ of 58 Senate seats).[23] Since there are very heavily urbanized counties upstate also, it would appear that any singularly urban-rural conflict would be resolved easily in favor of the urban interest. On the other hand, if legislators from all the 23 counties less than 40 percent urban combined with the 14 that are 40-49.9 percent urban, they would command only 37 votes in the Assembly and 11 of the votes in the Senate. Even so, this is a much more difficult combination to put together than the highly urbanized one. Yet if these legislators from the same 37 rural-urban counties were to combine; they would number among their constituents 2,081,986 urban residents, whereas if the legislators from the seven most urban counties were to combine— a much more likely prospect—they would number among their constituents a grand total of 63,883 rural residents. Which interest is likely to respect the minority more? If all legislators from all counties (32) having from 40 percent to 90 percent urban residents were to combine, they could only muster 50 votes in the Assembly and 22 7/10 in the Senate. Majorities are not easy to muster for any grouping of counties, but it would be fair to conclude that the New York City delegation should be in the best position of any population group as such to form a majority.

---

[23] "New York City with a population of 7,781,984 or 46% of the State's population of 16,782,304, has 65 assemblymen or 43.3% of the total assembly, and 25 senators or 43.1 of the total number of senators." WMCA v. Simon, U.S. Dist. Ct., 61 Civ. 1559 (1962), 4.

Proportional Representation

The advocates of reapportionment by the equal-populations principle are strangely quiet in regards to proportional representation. The probable explanation is amusing. Of all forms of apportionment, that involved in proportional representation of the kind commonly known and used in America conforms most exactly to the logic of the "one-man, one-vote" or "equal vote" doctrine.[24] For example, in 1892, John M. Berry in a book called *PR: The Gove System* declared: "Where citizens are equal—if ten men are to elect ten representatives, each man ought to elect one—if ten thousand are to elect ten representatives, each thousand ought to elect one." And, in truth, wherever PR is employed, almost all votes count in the election of officials. If a county has ten seats in the legislature and 1,000,000 voters, any 100,000 (actually less) voters that form behind a candidate can elect him. That is, the constituencies are "voluntary": they form themselves within the larger districts typically provided under PR. If the voters of City X numbered 5,000,000, and the whole State, including the City, 10,000,000, and a Senate of 50 were elected at large, the City could conceivably elect about 25 if it worked as a unity. Everybody's vote would count for somebody's election, a condition that does not exist under a majority or plurality election now nor would exist under any equal-populations reapportionment.

From the most authoritative survey and analysis of the effects of proportional representation in the government of modern states, we learn the following:

(1) Proportional representation is insensitive to normal variations in opinion and very sensitive to sudden mutations even when they are temporary and slight;

(2) The simple-majority single-ballot system is very sensitive to normal developments but insensitive to sudden mutations unless they are deep and lasting.[25]

---

[24] A. de Grazia, *Public and Republic, op. cit.,* 184-204.
[25] Duverger, *op. cit.,* 314.

In more concrete terms, the large shifts of seats from one party to another that occur under the typical election system in the States and Congress when only small shifts of opinion occur, do not happen under PR. But when any sizable group of the population is formed over an issue or a strong sentiment (such as could be metropolitan reform), that group opinion is quickly heard and felt in a legislature that is apportioned in part or all according to PR.

In fact, when political parties, personalities, issue-groups, and interest groups such as unions, farmers, or government employees would have displayed their effects, it is unlikely that anything more than a dozen of a "City bloc," agreed in a program for the City, would emerge. A great many other voters would have had other fish to fry in voting for candidates. Still, more leadership in pushing for a metropolitan program would emerge than exists at present or than would exist under reapportionment by equal-populations districts.

It may be concluded that the equal-populations advocates, unless they are majoritarians, should logically be espousing proportional representation. If their reply is that, since PR has a bad public image, they wish to settle for half-a-loaf, and therefore espouse equal-populations districts, then they must be regarded as advocates of special interests and they must logically accept a more split-up and volatile legislature.

If they are majoritarians in psychology, and numerologists as well, then they will not like PR. For all that proportional representation has a logic of numbers paralleling and going beyond equal-populations districts, it fosters group behavior that has meaningful and useful social consequences when contained. The equal-populations numerology, on the other hand, is a dangerous flirtation with mass neurosis. Man loses standing as a citizen— without regard to slogans of "one man, one vote"—when he is reduced to naked, abstract number. He has a faceless equality with other numbered citizens. They become equally devoid of group ties and human responsibilities until they become the mass. The "mass" in fact cannot be said to exist until citizenship has been destroyed through individuals being torn loose from their social relations and reduced to separate items, helplessly confronting the central state. That philosophical considerations such as these have weighed not at all against the numerology of so many courts and commentators should serve to warn Americans all the more of the ultimate issues involved in the events of these days. The astonishing swiftness with which even the most facile presentations of this image of man as number have been seized and acted upon in the present apportionment controversy suggests an appalling readiness to accept such an image of man as compelling and final, as axiomatic.

6.

THE REFORM OF APPORTIONMENT

AGITATION OVER REAPPORTIONMENT has been common for many years on the American political scene. It has taken the form of legislative conflict, of campaigns for public support, of group pressures, and of court proceedings. Something of the extent of the agitation in the past two years is indicated by the material of Chart IV. We are informed that in nine States prolonged debate has occurred on the reapportionment of congressional seats and in several cases deadlock has resulted. In 16 additional States, a mild or moderate interest within the legislature has been noted, while in 25 States no general interest was reported.

There was considerable interest concerning State apportionment in nine State legislatures, a mild interest in 24, and no interest noted in 17. However, the imperfections of the reporting are many. Only two sources were used, neither of which was intended to describe fully the agitation. For example, Michigan is carried in the "no interest noted" column whereas in fact the legal challenge to the very existence of the Michigan Senate caused one of the greatest domestic political crises of 1962. The press, the political organizations of the State, the candidates for State senatorial office and for the highest State offices, and the courts were in turmoil. But the legislature was not in session at the time. On the basis of rather tenuous deductions, I am inclined to believe that something between 5 and 10 percent of the typical legislator's "time on the job" is taken up with matters of elections and apportionment. Not more than several other legislative categories make so heavy a demand. Limiting reapportionment to once each 20 years would probably encourage more stable and significant relations between legislators and constituents.

Moving ahead, however, with our limited indicators of activity, we find that in 18 States the Governor was strongly involved in congressional or state legislative apportionment questions, and in 14 others was implicated in more limited activity. In four States a gubernatorial veto occurred on apportionment, but in half of the States, no interest was noted on the part of the Governor.

The reporting of court action is more complete. Since June 1960, litigation concerning apportionment has occurred in 25 State courts, and in federal courts involving 20 States. In 15 States, no litigation was noted. No particular quality seems to have preserved these States as a group from legal controversy.

Public Interest in Apportionment

In nine States a general public concern with problems of apportionment was reported. No doubt it would be of significance to
(Text continued on page 137)

CHART IV

OFFICIAL AND PUBLIC INTEREST IN THE APPORTIONMENT CONTROVERSY

	ALABAMA	ALASKA	ARIZONA	ARKANSAS	CALIFORNIA	COLORADO	CONNECTICUT	DELAWARE	FLORIDA	GEORGIA	HAWAII	IDAHO
I. INSTITUTIONAL INTEREST (RECENT)[a]												
A. EXTENT OF LEGISLATIVE INTEREST												
1. IN CONGRESSIONAL APPORTIONMENT												
a. SERIOUSLY DEADLOCKED, PROLONGED DEBATE[b]	X											
b. MUCH INTEREST, ALTHOUGH NO PROLONGED DEBATE				X	X		X		X			
c. MILD INTEREST, LITTLE, IF ANY DEBATE[c]			X									
d. NO INTEREST NOTED[d]		X				X		X		X	X	X
2. IN STATE LEGISLATIVE APPORTIONMENT												
a. SERIOUSLY DEADLOCKED, PROLONGED DEBATE												
b. MUCH INTEREST, ALTHOUGH NO PROLONGED DEBATE					X							
c. MILD INTEREST, LITTLE,,IF ANY, DEBATE[c]							X	X	X	X		
d. NO INTEREST NOTED[d]	X	X	X	X		X					X	X
B. EXTENT OF STATE EXECUTIVE INTEREST[e]												
1. STRONG LEADERSHIP[f]	X	X			•				X	X		
2. SOME, LIMITED ACTION				•	X							
3. VETOE OF BILLS	•											
4. NO INTEREST NOTED			• X	X		• X	X	X			X	• X
C. EXTENT OF JUDICIAL LITIGATION (SINCE JUNE, 1960)[g]												
1. IN STATE COURTS				X	X	X				X		X
2. IN FEDERAL COURTS	X				X	X		X	X	X		
3. NO LITIGATION NOTED		X	X				X				X	
II. PUBLIC INTEREST												
A. GENERAL HIGH PUBLIC INTEREST[h]	5			X	X	X		X	X			
B. SPECIFIC GROUP INTEREST[i]												
1. LABOR					X							
2. LEAGUE OF WOMEN VOTERS						X				X		
3. MUNICIPAL ASSOCIATIONS			[6] X	[7] X		[8] X						[9] X
4. OTHER												

	ILLINOIS	INDIANA	IOWA	KANSAS	KENTUCKY	LOUISIANA	MAINE	MARYLAND	MASSACHUSETTS	MICHIGAN	MINNESOTA	MISSISSIPPI	MISSOURI
I. INSTITUTIONAL INTEREST (RECENT)[a]													
A. EXTENT OF LEGISLATIVE INTEREST													
1. IN CONGRESSIONAL APPORTIONMENT													
a. SERIOUSLY DEADLOCKED, PROLONGED DEBATE[b]	X		X						X	X	X		X
b. MUCH INTEREST, ALTHOUGH NO PROLONGED DEBATE							[1] X	X				X	
c. MILD INTEREST, LITTLE, IF ANY DEBATE[c]				X	X								
d. NO INTEREST NOTED[d]		X				X							
2. IN STATE LEGISLATIVE APPORTIONMENT													
a. SERIOUSLY DEADLOCKED, PROLONGED DEBATE		X											
b. MUCH INTEREST, ALTHOUGH NO PROLONGED DEBATE			X					X			X		
c. MILD INTEREST, LITTLE,,IF ANY, DEBATE[c]				X	X	X						X	
d. NO INTEREST NOTED[d]	X						X		X	X			X
B. EXTENT OF STATE EXECUTIVE INTEREST[e]													
1. STRONG LEADERSHIP[f]	•	X			• X						•	X	•
2. SOME, LIMITED ACTION			X					X	X	X			
3. VETOE OF BILLS										•			
4. NO INTEREST NOTED	X			X		X	X						
C. EXTENT OF JUDICIAL LITIGATION (SINCE JUNE, 1960)[g]													
1. IN STATE COURTS		X	X	X	X			X	X	X	X	X	
2. IN FEDERAL COURTS		X			X	X			X	X			
3. NO LITIGATION NOTED	X						X						X
II. PUBLIC INTEREST													
A. GENERAL HIGH PUBLIC INTEREST[h]	X												
B. SPECIFIC GROUP INTEREST[i]													
1. LABOR			X						X	X			
2. LEAGUE OF WOMEN VOTERS		X	X					X	X				
3. MUNICIPAL ASSOCIATIONS		[10] X											
4. OTHER		[19] X	[20] X					[21] X	[22] X				

	MONTANA	NEBRASKA	NEVADA	NEW HAMPSHIRE	NEW JERSEY	NEW MEXICO	NEW YORK	NORTH CAROLINA	NORTH DAKOTA	OHIO	OKLAHOMA	OREGON
I. INSTITUTIONAL INTEREST (RECENT)[a]												
A. EXTENT OF LEGISLATIVE INTEREST												
1. IN CONGRESSIONAL APPORTIONMENT												
a. SERIOUSLY DEADLOCKED, PROLONGED DEBATE[b]												
b. MUCH INTEREST, ALTHOUGH NO PROLONGED DEBATE								X				
c. MILD INTEREST, LITTLE, IF ANY DEBATE[c]		X			X		X		X			
d. NO INTEREST NOTED[d]	X		X	X		X				[2] X	X	X
2. IN STATE LEGISLATIVE APPORTIONMENT												
a. SERIOUSLY DEADLOCKED, PROLONGED DEBATE												
b. MUCH INTEREST, ALTHOUGH NO PROLONGED DEBATE			X									
c. MILD INTEREST, LITTLE,,IF ANY, DEBATE[c]	X	X		X	X		X	X	X		X	X
d. NO INTEREST NOTED[d]						X				X		
B. EXTENT OF STATE EXECUTIVE INTEREST[e]												
1. STRONG LEADERSHIP[f]											X	X
2. SOME, LIMITED ACTION		•			X		X			X		
3. VETOE OF BILLS												
4. NO INTEREST NOTED	X	X	X	X		X		X	X			
C. EXTENT OF JUDICIAL LITIGATION (SINCE JUNE, 1960)[g]												
1. IN STATE COURTS				X	X				X		X	X
2. IN FEDERAL COURTS		X	X				X		X	X	X	
3. NO LITIGATION NOTED	X					X		X				
II. PUBLIC INTEREST												
A. GENERAL HIGH PUBLIC INTEREST[h]							X		X		X	
B. SPECIFIC GROUP INTEREST[i]												
1. LABOR	X						X					
2. LEAGUE OF WOMEN VOTERS							X		X		X	
3. MUNICIPAL ASSOCIATIONS	[11] X	[12] X					[13] X		[14] X	[15] X	[16] X	
4. OTHER												[23] X

	PENNSYLVANIA	RHODE ISLAND	SOUTH CAROLINA	SOUTH DAKOTA	TENNESSEE	TEXAS	UTAH	VERMONT	VIRGINIA	WASHINGTON	WEST VIRGINIA	WISCONSIN	WYOMING
I. INSTITUTIONAL INTEREST (RECENT)[a]													
A. EXTENT OF LEGISLATIVE INTEREST													
1. IN CONGRESSIONAL APPORTIONMENT													
a. SERIOUSLY DEADLOCKED, PROLONGED DEBATE[b]	X											X	
b. MUCH INTEREST, ALTHOUGH NO PROLONGED DEBATE													
c. MILD INTEREST, LITTLE, IF ANY DEBATE[c]											X		
d. NO INTEREST NOTED[d]		X	X	X	X	X	X	X	X	X			X
2. IN STATE LEGISLATIVE APPORTIONMENT													
a. SERIOUSLY DEADLOCKED, PROLONGED DEBATE			X									X	
b. MUCH INTEREST, ALTHOUGH NO PROLONGED DEBATE					X			X					
c. MILD INTEREST, LITTLE,,IF ANY, DEBATE[c]		X		X		X	[3] X		X		X		
d. NO INTEREST NOTED[d]	X									X			X
B. EXTENT OF STATE EXECUTIVE INTEREST[e]													
1. STRONG LEADERSHIP[f]	•	[4] X			X			X				X	
2. SOME, LIMITED ACTION									X		X		
3. VETOE OF BILLS							X					• X	
4. NO INTEREST NOTED	X		X	X		X	X			X			X
C. EXTENT OF JUDICIAL LITIGATION (SINCE JUNE, 1960)[g]													
1. IN STATE COURTS	X	X						X	X			X	X
2. IN FEDERAL COURTS					X				X	X		X	
3. NO LITIGATION NOTED			X	X		X	X				X		
II. PUBLIC INTEREST													
A. GENERAL HIGH PUBLIC INTEREST[h]													
B. SPECIFIC GROUP INTEREST[i]													
1. LABOR													
2. LEAGUE OF WOMEN VOTERS								X		X			
3. MUNICIPAL ASSOCIATIONS	[17] X								[18] X				
4. OTHER													

CATEGORY FOOTNOTES FOR CHART IV

"Official and Public Interest in the Apportionment Controversy"

a. Institutional interest is very difficult to objectively analyze. The data is based mainly upon an evaluation of reports in *Legislative Reapportionment in the States: A Summary of Action Since June, 1960* (Chicago: The Council of State Governments, 1962), and *Congressional Redistricting: Impact of the 1960 Census Reapportionment of House Seats* (Washington: Congressional Quarterly, No. 39, Part II, September 28, 1962).

b. Usually leading to protracted negotiations and compromise redistricting acts.

c. This category was employed where committees were formed to study the apportionment problem, where very limited action was taken, or where apportionment was almost a matter of automatic routine.

d. In most cases this category refers to States where no significant efforts were made to reapportion or redistrict.

e. Executive interest includes the actions of the Attorney General and other State officials as well as those of the Governor. References to this category mainly pertain to *State* apportionment matters. *Congressional* references are indicated by o.

(Thus o=only interest shown in congressional apportionment matters. x=only interest shown in State apportionment matters. x⁰=interest shown in both congressional and State matters.)

f. Includes calling a special session of the legislature, organizing meetings with citizens, being very outspoken on apportionment issues, etc.

g. Some of these suits have already been dismissed. Some are still pending.

h. It is very difficult to objectively evaluate general public interest. However, where certain types of behavior that manifest strong political interest were observed (e.g., heated political discussion, extensive press coverage of the issue, successful referendum petitions, etc.), this category was employed. An indication of interest is not meant to reflect any particular view of the apportionment problem.

i. Based upon groups mentioned in the references to the following category included in William J. D. Boyd (ed.), *Compendium on Legislative Apportionment* (New York: National Municipal League, 1962): "Organized current effort, if any, to alter the existing situation."

135

EXPLANATORY FOOTNOTES FOR CHART IV

*"Official and Public Interest
in the Apportionment Controversy"*

1. Democratic leaders threatened a referendum against the congressional redistricting bill.

2. Efforts to create a new congressional district were abandoned by the Republican controlled General Assembly. Two developments reportedly convinced Republicans that a new district was unnecessary or inadvisable: the death of George H. Bender, a former Representative and Senator, who had broken with the State Republican organization and announced his candidacy for an at-large seat in 1962; the opposition of Republican Representative Clarence J. Brown and other incumbent Congressmen, to the proposed redistricting plans.

3. The 1961 Utah legislature adopted a bill to reapportion itself on the basis of the 1960 census. This bill was vetoed by the Governor; the veto was sustained.

4. The Governor recommended reapportionment by the 1963 legislature. He named a study group and convened a special session of the R. I. General Assembly.

5. The public at large is "apathetic and disinterested," although reapportionment has "figured prominently in gubernatorial campaigns and in the legislative programs of several governors." (James E. Larson, "Alabama," *Compendium, op. cit.,* 2.)

6. The League of Arizona Cities and Towns.

7. "Officials of the Arkansas Municipal League do not normally—and as a matter of course—anticipate opposition of rural legislators to bills they sponsor to promote urban goals and interests." (Henry M. Alexander, "Arkansas," *ibid.,* 2.)

8. The Connecticut Public Expenditure Council

9. Associated Taxpayers of Idaho

10. Junior Chamber of Commerce, Indiana Municipal League

11. Montana Municipal League

12. The League of Nebraska Municipalities

13. The Citizens Committee for Fair Representation

14. Junior Chamber of Commerce

15. The Citizens League of Greater Cleveland

16. The Citizens for Constitutional Reapportionment

136

17. Citizens Committee for Fair Representation
18. The Committee of Seventy in Philadelphia
19. Indiana Civil Liberties Union
20. Iowa Citizens' Committee for a Constitutional Convention
21. The Maryland Committee for Fair Representation (a State-wide group)
22. The Massachusetts Federation of Taxpayer Associations
23. The Citizens Committee for Representative Government is sponsoring a constitutional amendment which would abandon the population standard for the Oregon House of Representatives and provide an area factor. The Bipartisan Committee to Retain Equal Representation is opposing this movement.

---

learn by elaborate research why these and not other States experienced public involvement; at first glance, they seem to have nothing that marks them off from the apathetic States, which are in the majority. Activities of labor unions are indicated in six States, and of the League of Women Voters in 11. Municipal associations entered the fray in 13 States, abetted by the National Municipal League, and several other interest groups were noted to be active in five States. Again the information must be considered fragmentary and incomplete.

When joined to other intelligence about the state of interest in apportionment around the country, it may be more reliably concluded that the public is generally apathetic and unaware of the nature of apportionment and of the issues involved in apportionment controversies. Everyone who has participated in apportionment campaigns agrees on this point. A passionate appeal for reapportionment, for instance, begins, "In a democracy, any action or condition which affects the right to vote is an important matter. It is puzzling, therefore, that unequal representation in the State legislature is not a subject to grip the interest and stir the emotions of the public."[1] The public is not far-sighted on special issues, perhaps. Or perhaps the judgment as to what is important is subjective; it can be argued that the question of equal-populations dis-

---

[1] James E. Larson, *Reapportionment and the Courts* (Bureau of Public Administration, University of Alabama, 1962), 1.

tricts is not important. And perhaps the number of people con· cerned with apportionment *is* average or more than average for legislative issues. If 5 percent of the electorate know of a State issue and have a general opinion about it, the issue should be considered exceptional. The work of State legislatures is shrouded in almost complete public apathy.

However, from time to time, the public is required to exhibit more activity because initiatives to reapportion are presented to it or referenda are placed before it. The response in these cases is not flattering to the proponents of apportionment changes.

In the 1952 general elections, the voters of Michigan were pre· sented with two proposed constitutional amendments relative to the apportionment of the State legislature. Both appeared on the ballot as the result of initiatives. One proposal provided for a Senate of 33 members elected from single member districts. The ratio for districting was the State population divided by 33, and no district might contain a greater than 15 percent deviation from this ratio. The House was to be of 99 members with the ratio calculated in the same way. Each Senate district was to contain three House districts. Reapportionment was to be by the Secretary of State each ten years, or, if he failed to act, by court proceedings. In short, a pure equal-populations district plan.

The succeeding proposal on the same ballot espoused a "federal principle." It placed the Senate on an area basis, with fixed districts described in the Constitution. The House was set at 110 members with the ratio computed by dividing the State population by 110. A county or group of counties received one representative if it had over 50 percent of the ratio, and another for each full ratio thereafter. The legislature was charged with decennial reapportionment, failing which the State Board of Canvassers might act. Here was, in brief, a contrasting plan weighted heavily in communities rather than individuals. It was also more complicated to explain.

The voters rejected the equal-populations districts plan by 1,415,355 to 924,242, a margin of 491,113. They accepted on the other hand the community-populations proposal by a vote of 1,269,807 to 975,518. Only two of the State's eight industrial coun ties favored the defeated proposal, the only two, in fact, of the State's 83 counties. Eighty-two percent of those voting for Governor voted on the first proposal, 79 percent on the second.

It was this winning proposition insofar as it concerned the Senate, and now incorporated in the Michigan Constitution, that was challenged before the courts in 1960 as being in violation of the equal protection and due process clauses of the 14th Amendment to the Federal Constitution. The State Supreme Court dismissed the petition, and the case was appealed. In April 1962, *Baker* v. *Carr* was decided, and the U.S. Supreme Court remanded the Michigan case for reconsideration in the light of *Baker* v. *Carr*. Meanwhile two judges had resigned and been replaced; the changes appeared to affect the position of the Court as a whole, for the challenged sections of the Michigan Constitution were now struck down in the light of *Baker* v. *Carr* in a 4-3 decision (July 18, 1962).[2] The prospective August 7 Senate Primary was voided, the legislature was given a month to redistrict, failing which all the Senators would run at large. In a chain reaction, the State's political processes developed into chaos. The Michigan Court refused to stay execution, but an appeal to Justice Stewart of the Supreme Court produced a delay and the elections proceeded according to the system established in 1952 by the popular referendum.

The Michigan case is a spectacular demonstration of how ideologies of the egalitarian-majoritarian type can leap quickly from adoration to contempt of the will of the citizens as expressed at the polls. The initiators of the equal-populations proposal defeated in the popular voting, and the plaintiffs seeking to declare the subsequent decision of the voters null and void were explicitly and overtly one and the same—the leaders of the Michigan State AFL-CIO. They called for an expression of the will of the people at the polls on the equal-populations proposal; when the "will of the people" did not conform to their plan, even those supposedly to benefit most opposing them, they turned to the courts in order to nullify the clear and unambiguous decision of the voters.

---

[2] Scholle v. Secretary of State, 367 Mich. 176 (1962).

Elsewhere in America, efforts at reapportioning by popular action have had only fair success. In seven States recently they have succeeded; in ten States they have failed (see Chart II).[3] It is unlikely too that the votes within legislatures would represent typically a minority of the population outside the halls. For instance, voting against reapportionment in the Washington State Senate on March 12, 1957 were 69 percent of the members whose constituents numbered 59 percent of the State population. General public opinion in apportionment matters, as in practically all political issues short of war and depression, moves by bits and pieces, adding or subtracting to the strength of the forces directly engaged in the political process.

The number of persons in any given State who know the details of its existing apportionment and any proposed new systems as well as something of the technique of accomplishing apportionment, would not ordinarily exceed a thousand—several hundreds of past or present legislators; a few legislative and executive staff members; a couple of judges; several journalists; a dozen professors; a hundred college students; and a hundred interest group representatives. This is the true public of State legislative apportionment. The federal public is most of these multiplied 50 times plus extra cohorts interested in national affairs. Many proud citizens would have to sympathize secretly with Governor Buford Ellington of Tennessee, ex-farm boy from Mississippi who, when asked about reapportionment, complained that he was "not smart enough" to have an answer.[4] When the subject is activated through a group drive with clearly opposed alternatives, the actual public increases to several thousands, and a mobilized response involving 80 percent of the presidential voters. (Cf. the Michigan 1952 case above.) It is not likely that a very considerable proportion of this 80 percent was at all familiar

---

[3] The best study available of a reapportionment movement involving the initiative and referendum is Gordon E. Baker's *The Politics of Reapportionment in Washington State* (New Brunswick, N. J., Eagleton Institute of Politics, 1960).

[4] *Nashville Tennessean*, June 14, 1961, which suggested that he might have been smart enough to avoid the issue. Cited by Wilder Crane, "Tennessee: Inertia and the Courts," in M. Jewell, ed., *The Politics of Apportionment* (New York, 1962), 318.

with the details of the proposals, but it was well understood which of the proposals constituted a threat to the community bases of apportionment. This public, however, deflates to ordinary size as soon as the issue is resolved.

The issue is often raised, in respect to apportionment, that the remedies available for change are inadequate. The problem has been dealt with in the section beginning on page 83. Obviously anarchy and chaos are the logical extremes of "political change made easy." The question has to be: "Can an 'urgent' problem backed by numerous and weighty political forces, find a solution through existing constitutional processes?" Fairly answered in the light of all other "urgent" problems, the answer would be "yes" in regards to practically all apportionment systems. For example, a basic ingredient of the democratic belief system calls for the informed participation of the public in public affairs. Yet we know that a small percentage of people are informed and interested in politics (perhaps 5 percent), while we act as if all were, justifying our fallacious presumption on grounds that, in an emergency, the people might well become interested. It is most difficult to impeach and convict a President on any constitutional grounds; do we abolish the provisions for the actions? Or do we make them easy to execute? A massive display of public opinion or a persistent determination on the part of "discriminated against" legislators ordinarily results in changes in the apportionment system. Referring again to the section beginning on page 83, the best proof of this supposition lies in the fact that reapportionment has occurred in almost all States since 1950.

Organization Activity

Non-governmental groups and city officials have stoked the fires of apportionment over a number of years. The principal agency has been the National Municipal League, composed of active citizens and local officials. Its monthly magazine, *National Civic Review,* is the organ for reapportionment forces. Some State and national labor union leaders, and various State chapters of the League of Woman Voters add their efforts to the movement to reapportion. Not to be

141

ignored is the influence of some large city newspapers, particularly *The New York Times,* a number of professors of political science, various political attorneys, and other activists scattered throughout the country.

The several organized interests involved are apparent. The National Municipal League has long sought greater attention to city demands and needs in State legislatures. Its officers, staff, and members share a profound conviction that the course of city government would be smoother if a numerical increment in legislative seats were to be obtained. Its program is broader than apportionment but never radical and rarely imaginative. It has scarcely encouraged research of a profound type into the dynamics of state-local relations, and to this day cannot offer, despite its unique observational advantages, a single first-class study of apportionment.

Nor have labor unions which are friendly to reapportionment on an equal-populations basis contributed more than simple activity. They have published, of course, a number of pamphlets reciting the well-known disproportions of population among different districts and urging the typical slogans of "equal representation." I can let Mary Goddar Zon, Research Director, AFL-CIO's Committee on Political Education since 1959, speak of the union contribution:

> The implications of the Supreme Court's decision in the Tennessee reapportionment case are salutary for labor. State legislative and congressional districts based on unequal divisions of the population have worked to devalue urban and metropolitan votes, including, of course, the votes of most trade union members. . . .
> Rural-dominated legislatures in many States have drawn congressional district lines in such a way as to repeat, as far as possible, the same pattern in the United States House of Representatives. As a result, the votes of a hundred or a thousand union members living in an urban district may have a par political worth no greater than a single vote in a rural district.[5]

---

[5] This is about the craziest single statistic I have encountered, although Morris Abram, a notable figure in reapportionment agitation declared in a New York speech that in 1961 "it took 159 college professors in Atlanta to equal the vote of one tenant farmer in the smallest Georgia county."

Labor has consistently supported proposed national legislation to require state legislatures to apportion United States Representatives' districts on the basis of population. State AFL-CIO officials have made the same appeal doggedly, year after year, before state legislative committees. . . . Resolutions have been passed on this subject repeatedly at state and national labor conventions, and reapportionment has been the subject of countless pamphlets, leaflets, and articles in the labor press.

Curiously, this was an issue which never before really caught the imagination of the membership. Even sophisticated unionists, quick to recognize and take vigorous action against a fast count in other areas, have been, in the main, singularly unmoved. If the courts had not opened an avenue of relief, it would be difficult to estimate when, or if, reapportionment might have emerged as a full-blown, mass-supported issue in labor ranks. This lethargy may have been attributable to despair of redress, since more concern has been evidenced in the months following the decision than in all the years preceding it.[6]

It should be added that the unions do not universally support reapportionment, apart from the question of their degree of enthusiasm for it. Where unions are located in areas that are "overrepresented" in the view of the equal-populations doctrine, they tend to favor the *status quo*. For example, in 1957 in Seattle, various labor precincts turned out a vote of 64.6 percent for redistricting while ten high-income conservative Republican precincts voted 82.3 percent for it. Central labor councils in Spokane and Everett opposed the initiative for reapportionment.[7]

There is a practical reason, too, why labor union leaders may be interested in apportionment by equal-populations districts, regardless of existing community boundaries. (It is understood that towns and cities can have seats proportioned to numbers without resorting to geometric districts.) Union leadership is easier to establish and maintain within a city, a metropolitan area, and a State if it can work up majorities directly, that is, which are not reflective of any intervening interests. Whether or not intended, an election district

---

[6] "Labor in Politics," *Law and Contemporary Problems* (Spring 1962), 250-51.

[7] Baker, *op. cit.,* 7.

based upon existing units of government tends to establish that unit as the interest base of the representative from the district. Any district paralleling a natural community does the same for that community. This effect resembles a "double-election," election of a representative to a legislature by a body once removed from the population. Lacking this effect, the representative has a perspective and a need of support that make him more vulnerable to unattached, general, and floating interest. These would tend to be interests such as labor unions which may be outside of the natural networks of power that govern the typical community.[8]

Support of Existing Apportionments

We have already shown that the existing apportionments are hardly in want of popular support, when that support becomes an issue. Further, much is wrong with the belief that constitutional conventions are stacked invariably against equal-population districts. A study of the Arizona Constitutional Convention of 1910 by David Bingham shows, for instance, that the five most populous counties could have commanded the Convention and introduced equal-population districts. "But they didn't. There isn't even any indication that a serious move in this direction was attempted."[9] The traditional, the customary, the federal example, and the play of interests and regions took precedence over the doctrine of equal-numbers.

Nor do existing systems of apportionment in the States and Congress lack organized support. Farmer associations are obviously friendly in most cases to the disapportionment number of seats provided to the less urbanized sections of every State and the nation. Their influence in apportionment, as in legislation generally, is less than it used to be. In fact, it is probably improper to regard the struggle over apportionment any more as a primarily rural-urban

---

[8] Cf. Zon, *op. cit.,* 237, where are described the beginnings of COPE activity to "develop organizational techniques coordinating the activities of existing COPE's across geographical or political boundaries" in cities and suburbs.

[9] "Legislative Apportionment: The Arizona Experience," *Arizona Review,* October 1962, 6.

struggle; in most places it is not rural interests at all but people from a cluster of smaller urban interests who are opposing interests from the largest cities of the jurisdiction. Yet the farmers and their agents must be counted on behalf of the *status quo,* even though the direct representation-equal populations doctrine was developed by and for farmers in the early days of the struggle for popular rule.

Besides the farm groups must be numbered the rather solid sentiments on behalf of community representation and against metropolitan power held by the network of power in the towns and small cities. In addition, many large and small business interests of the metropolis prefer the *status quo* because they are enabled to find compatible views among the legislators of smaller areas.[10] This is not always true and has not been so true in the past, when the sources of anti-business agitation and regulation have been rural populism such as the Greenbackers and the Populists. But the farm and town people and their representatives are still ideologically *laissez-faire* to an extent impossible among city legislators. The unions are primary factors in insisting upon instructed voting over a wide range of issues inimical to business and commercial interests. The resort for representation is naturally the farms and towns where, apart from a set of views governing the promotion of farm life, the representatives can be freer agents and lend a readier ear to the case brought by business.

In politics, every interest takes its support where it finds it, and defends its interests as far as it can. Constitutions and legislation are practical schemes, if they are to work. They measure and evaluate social interests and social forces. If they are to be reformed, they have to be intelligently and realistically reformed. The interests involved have to be considered fully. It is not to be expected that everyone will stand by politely when the League of Women Voters decides upon reapportionment as its national project and suggests that its members go to work redrawing the district lines of the States.

The reasons why legislators are loath to reapportion are numerous and are not too well understood. As Professor Malcolm E. Jewell puts it: "The only argument for change is the need for population

---

[10] Cf. fn. 18, Chart III.

equality, and to most legislators—even those from underrepresented areas—this argument appears highly theoretical and devoid of practical advantage." [11] Reapportionment is popular with few members of the legislatures. This fact surprises people who think that only legislators who might lose their own seats are against it. But the typical legislator suffers from the long proceedings; the need to guard himself against too much tampering with his own boundaries; the need to lose thousands of known constituents and to acquire thousands more who are completely unknown; the need to reorganize associational ties of many kinds with churches, union locals, businessmen, clubs, and the like; the necessary struggle for power with other legislators with whom he had hitherto been at peace; the need to read new newspapers; perhaps a change in his own home address; the possibility of increased risk of losing his seat; the need to shuffle his staff around to accommodate new interests and drop old; the need to reconsider his factional alignments in the legislature; the need to familiarize himself with new units of government, new school districts, and all their legislative needs. The list is only partial. It is only fair to compare it with the breaking up and reorganizing of a business office or a factory. When labor unions will strike to keep another worker from touching a wire that "belongs" to their craft, or a community will exert its maximum efforts to have all levels of government restrain an army camp from leaving their area, or a council of professors will resist any attempt to change the courses they must teach, there are any number of sympathetic experts on human relations to explain their position and ease their situation. Who does this for the legislators? They too are a human community.

The State legislatures, which had been treating problems of apportionment much as they had for a century or more, were shocked into defensive activity by judicial threats. A spectrum of responses to *Baker* v. *Carr* was exhibited. These amounted to speeding up reapportionments, and decreasing population differences among districts in extreme cases. The dismay among legislators was great, while exuberance of the equal-populations advocates after *Baker* v. *Carr*

---

[11] In Jewell, ed., "Political Patterns in Apportionment," *The Politics of Apportionment* (New York: Atherton Press, 1962), 28.

was unrestrained. In the haste demanded by the courts there was little opportunity given for a principled and substantial defense, so convinced were most legislators that the ax had fallen. "The Road to Chaos!" headlined the *State Journal* of Michigan after the second Michigan case. "Chaos—by Court Order" exclaimed *The Detroit News*. Unfamiliar cases and legal doctrines were handed to State legal officers. Legislatures and governors who were unused to cooperating except at a snail's pace were thrown together for emergency decisions and sessions. It might have been a rehearsal for civil defense.

The Wisconsin legislature tangled with the Governor in an exchange of bills and vetoes, and the situation there was saved only by a brilliant Special Master, appointed by the court to straighten out the problems it had itself engendered in connection with a State legislature not hostile but indeed high in the favor of equal-populations advocates and failing by only a year its duty to reapportion the State. Here and elsewhere, governors and other executive officers of the States became involved because they could not avoid action when the State's legal officers had to contest legal actions brought against the State, or because a political struggle erupted.

The courts have not removed the apportionment problem from politics. They have in fact greatly stimulated political controversy, as in Michigan, New York, Georgia, and Wisconsin. Whether the court-induced uproar is only temporary and will be succeeded by a less controversial, a calmer and more orderly situation in the long run cannot be surely predicted. For the time being, Justice Frankfurter's dire forebodings of political confusion seem to have been borne out by events. The calm, if and when it comes, may be the calm of death for federalism.

7.

CONSTITUTIONAL AUTHORITIES

The moment is appropriate now to ask who shall determine the law of apportionment. If an apportionment is always in favor of some set of interests, who is to say what interests shall be favored? The answer is handed us by universal and historical practice; *the constitutional authorities that set up the system of representative government should determine the base of apportionment.* It is the only possible answer in a constitutional order. For the alternative answer is that the base of apportionment should be determined by whoever wishes to do so, and has the power.

The Informed Consensus on Judicial Objectivity

The problem of defining constitutional authorities, is, of course, difficult; but it is not so difficult as to have excused the disorderly spectacle in the courts and politics of the country in these past months. Constitutional authority is the ultimate source to which the justification of governmental action is referred. In the present case we must speak of the usual hierarchy of authorities of American law: the Federal Constitution; the amendments to the Constitution; and the determinations of the federal courts on questions arising out of litigation; the State constitutions; and the decisions of State courts.

Any contradictions that may arise are decided in favor of the superior authority. Such is the accepted and legitimate legal principle. Many lawyers and professors may be more learned, exact and rational than the judges, but the rules of the order say that the judges' determinations of law alone are valid.

However, although the judges' determinations are accepted by the political order as law, the judges themselves are parties to an issue which cannot be resolved irresponsibly by themselves. Such is the issue of the objectivity of the law. The objectivity of law we define as that idealized condition when all informed and reasonable persons agree that the application of a law to a case does not deviate from previous applications to similar cases except by the rules of empirical and deductive logic.[1] The objectivity of the law is the ultimate condition served by the operating principle: "A judge does not make the law; he only applies it."

To the degree to which judges vary in a decision or class of decisions from this principle, they become non-judicial. When the deviation becomes extensive in the eyes of a great many who make up *the informed consensus on objectivity,* judges are bound by the nature of their office and function to reduce their deviance, what-

---

[1] I am aware that this model deviates farther from the reality of judicial decision-making than other models that intend to make a "best-fit" with reality, as e.g., Edward Levi in *Introduction to Legal Reasoning,* (Chicago, 1949). But my model is meant to be of an ideal form for organizing and directing preferences.

ever their personal belief or will. In this sense, a judge is responsible, and must remain constantly so or risk imperiling the constitutional order and the rule of law. The judge can be, and if necessary must be, a minority of one against the world in applying the law. He can only be, and necessarily must be, a member of the informed consensus on objectivity when he makes law. On occasion, a judge, depending largely upon the urgency of the condition of which the case at hand is typical, and upon the priority given that condition in the total constitutional order, should make law. But to assert that this function has no bounds except those of the political philosophy of the judge, or of even the associated judges of a court at a given time, can only result in the deterioration of the constitutional order and the reduction of constitutional authority to questions of immediate power.

Fitting Baker v. Carr to the Constitution

More than in the early days of State government, apportionment systems are today contained in State constitutions. There is no conceivable challenge to this right of the States except insofar as the Federal Constitution and federal law are invoked. In matters of apportionment, then, that doctrine which "should" prevail can cut some path outdoors but cannot enter unless incorporated into a constitutional doctrine. The possibilities are several:

1. Apportionment can be arranged to suit the wishes of the constitutional authorities of the State.
2. Apportionment must be by equal-populations districts, whatever the State constitutional authorities may desire.
3. Apportionment must pay some heed to population, whatever the State constitutional authorities may desire.
4. *Apportionment can be arranged in any way that the State constitutional authorities desire unless the Federal Constitution is violated.*

American constitutional law requires the fourth way. Some certain clauses of the Federal Constitution must be in conflict with the apportionment formula of the State constitution in order for it to be null and void. If the conflict is not flagrant or intended we cannot be sure of its existence and are thrown upon the mercies of the courts to judge factually and wisely the nature of the conflict. In so judging, the courts are not legally entitled to regard their constitutional position as superior to that of the States in any other way than that of having a final power to define the line between State and federal. In every other way, it is possible, proper, and legal to assert that State government is of an importance and status equal to, if not greater than, the Supreme Court.

It is believed, with some reason, by persons presently engaged in the controversy over reapportionment in America, that the meanings of the Negro integration cases stimulated application of the 14th Amendment to apportionment problems.[2] This belief warrants analysis, even if we must shift into the form of reasoning used on the instable sands of the equal-protection concept.

Chronologically, the development took the following form: Prior to the Brown Case,[3] the Supreme Court appeared to maintain that the requirement of equal education for Negroes and whites met the constitutional requirement of equal-protection if it were equal-but-separate. In the Brown case, equality in education was deemed to require integration of education of whites and Negroes. In other words, a tight equality, barring practically any classification by race, was imposed. This went contrary to a broad tendency in economic and social matters to permit *loose* equality, with a great many discriminatory classifications.[4]

Not long afterwards, the Alabama legislature, in a racist maneuvre of the type that costs "States Rights" grave losses, gerrymandered the population of Tuskegee, to minimize the electoral

---

[2] Cf. Ruth Silva, "Legislative Representation," *op. cit.,* 429: "Since the segregation cases have so greatly extended the scope of the equal protection clause of the fourteenth amendment, the strength of the *Colegrove* precedent has been repeatedly challenged." The weakening of the separate-but-equal doctrine was perceptible years before *Brown.*

[3] Brown v. Board of Education, 347 U.S. 483 (1954).

[4] Stanley Friedelbaum, *"Baker v. Carr:* The New Doctrine of Judicial Intervention . . ." *University of Chicago Law Review,* Summer 1962.

power of the Negroes there. This legislation was struck down as an unconstitutional denial of the right of suffrage under the 15th Amendment in the case of *Gomillion* v. *Lightfoot.*[5]

The conjunction of the apportionment issue in the Gomillion case with the strict interpretation of equality in the Brown case may have triggered the reasoning of one or more Justices in *Baker* v. *Carr,* and would also seem to have excited the advocates of "equal representation," [6] For if discrimination against the most populous areas could be proven, and could be validly compared with discrimination against Negroes, and if one form of malapportionment was of the same illegal character as another, then the whole structure of legislative apportionment in America could be assaulted.

This reasoning can be psychologically explained but is not logically and empirically tenable. In the first place, there is explicit constitutional language giving equal rights to Negroes and voiding discrimination on grounds of race. Secondly, the showing of cause for action is much easier and clearer in cases of general discrimination against Negroes; the probable effect is more separable from other questions. Thirdly, the structure of federalism is not threatened by the National Government's actions in the cases of Negro discrimination. (However, extreme resistance to federal government action, itself provoked by federal measures against discrimination, might injure the basis of States Rights in public opinion, law, and practice.) Fourthly, the pace of change in the law of race relations has been much slower than the rate of change in reapportionments. Fifth, the settlement of problems of discrimination against Negroes is of paramount national and international importance. Finally, the inequality being considered is intense and personal in the

---

[5] 364 U.S. 339 (1960). Justice Whittaker, concurring, argued that the decision should have been based on the equal protection clause of the 14th Amendment.

[6] Anticipatory action in this regard came with the Hawaiian case of Dyer v. Kazuhisa Abe, 138 F. Supp. 220 at 224 (1956), where the federal district court stressed the *Brown* case and declared: "Any distinction between racial and geographic discrimination is artificial and unrealistic: both should be abolished." I, of course, regard this distinction as both "natural" and "realistic."

152

racial case, and diffuse and impersonal in the general apportionment case. To compare the distress and weakness of the Negroes with that alleged to be the case with regard to city-dwellers owing to apportionment is absurd to the point of impertinence. To those who defend the comparison, we should say: "To qualify for judicial intervention, prove experiences like these: Go into slavery for a hundred years. Suffer through a civil war. Be denied the elementary rights of citizens for another century. Then come before us cloaked in the equal protection clause of the 14th Amendment. We should then respond that you certainly are entitled to such protection, and if the 14th Amendment did not exist, we should have to invent it. But without anything like this in the history of apportionment, there is no need for judicial invention."[7]

Some State courts have been charged with the review of apportioning procedures for years. Mr. Arthur L. Goldberg has cited 54 cases in which apportionments were invalidated, prior to *Baker* v. *Carr*.[8] There is even a smattering of theory about representation and apportionment to be found in court decisions going back to earliest times. At the same time, almost all of these cases may be shown to be highly tentative and apologetic incursions into the province of the legislature.[9] Unless ordered by law, or unless the issue at hand is clearly of a judicial nature, State courts have been loath to clash with the legislatures. They, like the Supreme Court until lately, have been wary of the jurisdictional and political implications of such cases. The federal courts, except in two aborted instances, have

---

[7] The great failures of integration have been of a purely political character and rest with the politicians of the country. Cf. A. de Grazia, "A New Way Towards Equal Suffrage," *New York University Law Review,* April 1959, 716. This author agrees that the Court must have faced its responsibilities in the segregation cases. He disagrees with the method of judicial intervention chosen, believing desegregation could have been instituted from the bottom of the educational ladder upwards with greater orderliness.

[8] "The Statistics of Malapportionment," *Yale Law Journal,* November 1962, 102-3.

[9] Robert G. Dixon, Jr., "Legislative Apportionment and The Federal Constitution," XXVII *Law and Contemporary Problems,* 1962, 332-39.

done the same. But, as Chart II shows, once charged by the Supreme Court, both court systems undertook vigorous action.

The relevant specific determination of *Baker* v. *Carr* was that the apportionment-in-effect in Tennessee, which was alleged to be in violation of the Tennessee Constitution's formula of apportionment based on population and was not kept up to date with changes in population, was therefore conceivably in violation of the 14th Amendment of the Federal Constitution, which imposes upon the State the guarantee to all persons within their jurisdiction of the equal protection of the laws. There Justice Brennan delivered the opinion of the Court. Justices Douglas, Clark, and Stewart wrote separate concurring opinions, and Justices Frankfurter and Harlan each wrote dissenting opinions in which the others joined.

The least disputable general determination of the Supreme Court in *Baker* v. *Carr* appears to have been that State apportionment systems, whether contained in the State constitution or in legislation, could be admitted to examination in a case before a Federal Court to determine whether they violate the equal-protection provision of the 14th Amendment of the Federal Constitution. Prior to the case, the Court had refused to admit apportionment systems except when racial discrimination was alleged (and shown) to be the basis for a particular apportionment in Alabama (*Gomillion* v. *Lightfoot*). Relying upon precedents such as *Colegrove* v. *Green* (328 U.S. 549 [1946])[10] the Court had appeared to consider apportionment an integral government function, interference with which would constitute an abridgment of the separation of powers and of the federal system. Yet all along, it can be shown, the Court has disturbed States' constitutions and structures of government (school systems and election systems, for example) where a violation of a federal right had occurred.

It appears, therefore, that the Court, in *Baker* v. *Carr*, was adopting this approach to apportionment systems. This would appear to be a necessary implication of the role of the federal courts in the federal system. As we have demonstrated in this work, not

---

[10] These cases are listed in Baker v. Carr (30 LW 4228, March 26, 1962).

only the suffrage, but every device of representative government can be made to incorporate different and opposed preferences about human conduct and public policy; this is true of race, occupation, party, and many other human distinctions. The Court would then forego its primary mission of defense of the Constitution were it to draw back from questions of apportionment.

However, the very logic of the admission of apportionment systems to the jurisdiction of the federal courts must exclude any notion that an arbitrary apportionment system is called for. Since an essential reason for admitting apportionment systems to court scrutiny has to be that the same sort of politiking can be done with apportionment devices as with devices and methods of voting and suffrage, then by the same token varied forms of apportionment must be acceptable.

Litigation on apportionment occurred in 21 States between *Baker* v. *Carr* (March 26, 1962) and December 11, 1962. In Michigan, Florida, and Georgia, State constitutional provisions were voided. The adjoining table, based on a reading of the cases, reveals that all 12 court decisions ordering reapportionment action used a theory based largely on the equal-populations doctrine as a major justification. In three States, the courts rejected pleas for reapportionment, but only one can be definitely said to pay no regard to the doctrine. This was the New Hampshire Court. The New York Federal District Court might possibly be deemed to have rejected the doctrine. In two of the six States where a final decision has not come, a population standard was set. Thus with one or two exceptions, the courts, far from being tempered by the words of Justice Stewart, have plunged heavily towards an extreme interpretation of *Baker* v. *Carr* and are making the egalitarian doctrine into law.

There are many statements and implications in *Baker* v. *Carr* that numerical regimentation of a system of representation is uncalled for. If the only determinant of the representative and democratic quality of a government institution were its numerical relations to the public, the greater part of all American, federal, State, and local governments would be revolutionized. While the House of Representatives is apportioned in large part by the principle of equal districts (but note the several exceptions, including a basic single seat regardless of population, respect for State boundaries in the allotment of seats and voting as State blocs in the House in the case of a presidential election bound over from the Electoral College for lack of a majority there, etc.) it is countered by the Senate, the Electoral College, the federal judiciary with its many apportioned field districts, the executive establishment with its many agencies of many apportioned field offices—including a number of elective functional constituencies such as the agricultural production control and soil conservation system—and the numerous independent agencies with all their powers and no electorates at all. For it is logical that "equality" be provided in elective but not in appointive apportionments? Then would come the States with the same situations, and then the local governments, perhaps a hundred thousand of which would need reapportioning, both for elective and appointive bodies.[11]

There can be little doubt that the process will stop short of this. It can readily do so if the opinion of the Supreme Court in *Baker* v. *Carr* be understood simply to say that the constitutional authorities must introduce some principle of democracy into their government whereby it can be symbolized and demonstrated that all of the people are at the source of the governments and are entitled to involve themselves in the control and direction of public affairs. The suffrage is by all odds the most significant symbol and instrument to this end but certainly the conditions for the use of the vote must be maintained, among them a significant degree of leverage so that opinions may find their way to the centers of government.

If this criterion is adopted, it is probable that only one or two State constitutional apportionments would be deemed to violate the Federal Constitution. The results will still be important. First, potential attacks upon minorities through apportionment machinery

---

[11] For example, about 200 counties apportion county board members to the towns and townships. In several States, some county board members are appointed by other officials. Some county boards are composed of justices of the peace. Most counties elect board members from districts. Alfred de Grazia, *American Way of Government* (New York: Wiley, 1957), 847-8.

Table V.

JUDICIAL USE OF EQUAL-POPULATIONS DOCTRINE IN LITIGATION SINCE *BAKER* v. *CARR**

(Cases in which the doctrine was a major or considerable element in the Court's decision)

State	Case	Pro-Reapportionment		Anti-Reapportionment	
		Because of Equal-pop. Doctrine	Other Criteria	Because Equal-Pop. Doctrine Not Violated or Not Violated Enough	Because no Invidious Discrimination Proven or no Standard for Proving Such
Ga.	Toombs v. Fortson	x			
Ala.	Sims v. Frink	x			
Tenn.	Baker v. Carr	x			
Okla.	Moss v. Burkhart	x			
Vt.	Mikell v. Rousseau	x			
R. I.	Sweeney v. Notte	x			
Mich.	Scholle v. Hare	x			
Kan.	Harris v. Shanahan	x			
Miss.	Fortner v. Barnett	x			
Va.	Mann v. Davis[1]	x			
Fla.	Sobel v. Adams, Swann v. Adams	x			
N. Y.	WMCA v. Simon			(x)[2]	
Idaho	Caesar v. Williams			x	
N. H.	Levitt v. Attorney General				x
Md.	Maryland Committee for Fair Representation v. Tawes	x			
Wisc.	Wisconsin v. Zimmerman	(Final Decision Reserved or Pending)			
N. D.	State *ex rel.* Lein				
Neb.	League of Nebraska Municipalities v. Marsh	,,	,,	,,	,,

Table V. continued

State	Case	Pro-Reapportionment		Anti-Reapportionment	
		Because of Equal-pop. Doctrine	Other Criteria	Because Equal-Pop. Doctrine Not Violated or Not Violated Enough	Because no Invidious Discrimination Proven or no Standard for Proving Such
Colo.	Stein v. General Assembly of State of Colorado & Lisco v. McNicholas	,,	,,	,,	,,
Cal.	Silver v. Jordan	,,	,,	,,	,,
Pa.	Start v. Lawrence v. Sathre	,,	,,	,,	,,

*Despite the Justice Stewart clarification of the majority opinion in Baker v. Carr.

[1] U.S.Dist.Ct. E. Va., 31 *U.S. Law Week,* November 28, 1962, 2263. (Stayed by Chief Justice Warren on December 16, 1962.)

[2] However, the Court made the question of "invidious discrimination" the paramount one.

will be discouraged. Second, denials of popular access to legislative and conciliar bodies in existing or contemplated systems will be frustrated.

On the other hand it is also probable that various instances of gross legislative violation of State constitutional provisions regarding apportionment will be visited by federal judicial sanctions. Failure to apportion and malapportionment—that is, failure to carry out State constitutional provisions on apportionment and deliberate violation of such provisions—may be regarded as possible denials of equal protection of the laws. The logic here is clear: constitutional authority sets and defines rights, including the right to republican (representative) government; the devices of representative government, once so defined, are parts of a constitutional rule of law; actions in violation of these rights, besides being unconstitutional in relation to a State constitution, might be construed to violate the

Federal Constitution's guarantees of a republican form of government, due process of law, and equal protection of the laws. Severe malapportionment and outrageous failure to execute the law of the State constitution amount to tampering with the basic structure of the government; they are a breach of an expected and depended-upon regularity in the legal system and consist of consciously enabling some people in a State to gain certain advantages over others that otherwise had been denied them by superior law.

Transferring to legal language, we are confronted with that constitutional principle called "justiciability." An issue that is not justiciable cannot be adjudicated, the doctrine goes. And what is justiciable is defined by the Supreme Court as whatever will not embarrass the Court or the country politically and whatever can be handled by court decision without making a botch of affairs. It may be useless to reargue *Baker* v. *Carr* on this concept; perhaps in no set of cases has the Court been so beset by illogic as in those taking up justiciability. One might read Justice Brennan's ruling opinion in *Baker* v. *Carr* and conclude that he is·making a powerful case for non-justiciability. For he asserts a sweeping political power of the Supreme Court to dictate the form of State government; and the precedents he ascribes to his opinion are full of dread of consequences, and appear to support the position of the State of Tennessee.

This study has consistently maintained that a question of State apportionment systems may be justiciable, but it is justiciable only under extreme conditions incorporating in effect the constitutional provision that guarantees republican government in the States, or else under a particular unconstitutional wrong to a party, such as racial discrimination. Since so many substantive conditions are created by any apportionment system, many of them minor in nature, it is absolutely necessary to determine in any case who is being helped by the apportionment at issue and who will be gratuitously helped or harmed by the imposition of an alternate system. Lacking such specificity the courts, maintaining as they now must that many parties can have standing in apportionment cases and that such cases are justiciable, should dismiss for failure to show injury.

These then, we think, should be the limits of the federal judicial position. It is apparent that a new and important stance is to be expected. However, the danger to the guarantees of republican government to the States and of State rights, to due process of law and to the logic of the "equal protection" concept is great indeed if certain other dicta of the Court opinions in *Baker* v. *Carr* are made law and if the widespread agitation for districts of equal populations is allowed to succeed.

To take away from the constitutional authorities of a State (beginning with its very constitutional convention and its constitution) the right to determine the character of its representative system would be a powerful blow against American federalism.[12] For the Supreme Court, itself unelective, to demolish partially the representative structure of the States on some wholly inferred and rarely practical doctrine of "equal-populations districts" would be the crowning irony in the history of judicial law-making. Neither the judicial power nor the force of the Federal Constitution is weakened if it is acknowledged clearly and explicitly that the structure of representative government can be as unique and flexible as the genius of the State authorities can provide.

---

[12] I can only deal cursorily here with the question whether it is practical for the federal or State courts to enter upon reapportionment tasks. That the tasks are difficult is indubitable. Still, possibly as complicated cases have arisen in connection with tax, antitrust, and other matters, where the courts have had to prepare plans and oversee their administration. Moreover, to remedy failures to reapportion and malapportionment, the courts must enter this area. What can be said of this problem can be said more generally of government, namely that the courts are irrational in facing their policymaking tasks. The necessary fictions of judicial neutrality and non-legislation must be firmly upheld, but some system can be contrived for permitting more elaborate preliminary research and post-observations of behavior in cases that make policy. The use of a qualified Special Master, as in Wisconsin, is one way, provided such a person is not in effect made into a one-man constitutional convention. Direct studies authorized by the court and delegated to outside agencies are another means. All are regrettable substitutes for action by the legislatures, and their research and intelligence instruments.

Predicting the outcome of cases pending before the Supreme Court is not recommended, unless necessary. A single Justice's vote can turn the course of law one way or another. Justice Frankfurter, a brilliant dissenter in *Baker* v. *Carr,* has been replaced by Justice Goldberg. Some will say that this change may reinforce the extended interpretation of that decision. Still Justices change upon appointment. The prespectives of incumbent Justices change, too. The Chief Justice, whose words were not directly registered in the majority opinion of *Baker* v. *Carr,* as Governor of California once said: "I have always believed that rural counties are of much more significance in the life of our state than the population those counties would represent . . . and I believe the principle of balanced representation in the two houses of the legislature is in keeping with the federal system of representation.[13]

Nor is there any compulsion on the Court to choose the "rational" way preferred by the observer. Therefore let us set forth what logic should be and might be operative within the Court on apportionment.[14]

---

[13] Quoted in Thomas S. Barclay, "The Reapportionment Struggle in California in 1948," *Western Political Quarterly,* June 1951, 319.

[14] For comparative purposes, the following editorial is reproduced. It indicates the kind of combined propaganda, wild wishing, and dubious jurisprudence that has been aroused by Baker v. Carr.

"As the first months of activity are evaluated, it is well to take a look at the nation-wide consequences of *Baker* v. *Carr.* My analysis is:

"1. The people know they need no longer suffer from archaic unrepresentative state government.

"2. State legislatures know that unless they reapportion themselves fairly the courts will do so.

"3. Reapportioned state governments will become more effective parts of our governmental machinery.

"4. The oft-repeated words 'states' rights' will not assume real meaning as states begin again to exercise their governmental powers.

"5. Unshackling of long dormant state powers will enable urban problems to be dealt with at state capitals with lessened reliance upon Washington.

The Court will be strongly impelled to limit severely the scope of *Baker* v. *Carr* as precedent, for the following reasons:

1. It should now be apparent to the Court that Justice Frankfurter was right in stressing the unavoidably political character of every element of the apportionment process, including the doctrine of equal-populations.

2. The Court should now be fully aware of the existence of equally valuable historical traditions that do not incorporate the equal-populations doctrine.

3. The Court should appreciate, in view of 1 and 2 above, the "acceptable rationality" of perhaps every scheme of apportionment in existence today.

4. The Court should be aware of the numerous ways in which cities and majorities can rule without the instruments that in many cases have been specifically denied them.

5. The Court can understand more clearly now the distinction between apportionment and malapportionment—the first being gov-

---

"6. Cities after decades of denials and frustrations will have the votes to secure essential home rule powers to meet local needs.

"7. It is certain that archaic state legislative machinery will now be modernized.

"8. Genuine state constitutional reform is now possible.

"9. The extensive nation-wide dialogue on the fundamentals of our system of government provides an opportunity to restudy and reallocate public powers and functions to those levels of government best able to perform them under twentieth century conditions.

"10. Even the doubters who depreciated the effectiveness of court jurisdiction must now concede it has been dramatically effective.

"EDITOR'S NOTE.—This guest editorial is made up of excerpts from an address before a joint session of the National Municipal League and the American Political Science Association, September 8, by CHARLES S. RHYNE, past president of the American Bar Association and general counsel of the National Institute of Municipal Law Officers, who was of counsel in the significant *Baker v. Carr* case." (*National Civic Review,* October 1962, 481).

ernmental by constitutional authority, the second being misgovernment by abuse of or failure to observe the law. Precedents and logic alike permit one to assert constitutionality of a legal set (X_L) in jurisdiction (A) which, if it were an illegal set (X_I) in jurisdiction (B) would be unconstitutional. A right against a statute need not be a right against a constitution.

6. The States can be shown to have acted at a reasonable pace in accomplishing apportionment. The cutting-off point at which a system becomes impossible to amend has been too hastily adjudged.

7. The States have already accomplished changes, even if *in terrorem;* additional extensive, concrete action is not necessary.

8. The difficulties of accomplishing apportionment by judiciary are more apparent than ever.

9. The contradictions of a non-popular Court pursuing abstract psychological equality by denying numerous sorts of freedom to 50 working governments must be of some concern.

10. The absence of proof of unconstitutional legislative injury to petitioners in apportionment cases is a serious defect in the merits of their case.

11. The courts can also be brought to see that from the standpoint of a federal system of government, any extension of the doctrine of *Baker* v. *Carr* will be a shocking assault on the legislative competence of the States.

12. The courts can also be shown that a great many possibly beneficial schemes of apportionment and representation for the future will be blocked if the U.S. Constitution is read to mean equal-populations disfricts must be the universal or even dominant mode of apportionment.

13. Furthermore, the courts may realize that making into law the doctrine of equal-populations and equal-representation will logically extend a destructive impulse towards a hundred thousand other government entities and to practices of national, State, and local governments alike.

14. Nor should there now be any question in the Court's mind about the vast difference that exists betwen this whole range of cases and subjects and the obviously constitutional status of race relations.

15. The Court may well observe that, in the guise of dispensing mechanical and abstract equality, it is actually swinging a heavy political power on behalf of definable and recognizable contestants of numerous types in the American political scene.

For all of these reasons, the courts should not and are unlikely to extend the meaning of *Baker* v. *Carr* beyond that of a "shotgun over the door." The legislatures in turn would be ill-advised to retreat from their fundamentals.

8.

FUTURE APPORTIONMENT

THE JUDICIAL ACTIVITY now occurring with respect to apportionment has within it the potential to damage constitutionalism and federalism,[1] but not to do more than correct some wrongs of malap-

---

[1] The author's definitions, analysis, and viewpoint of constitutionalism and federalism are contained in *State-Federal Relations,* report of the first (Hoover) Commission on Organization of the Executive Branch of Government, on whose staff he served as Consultant; *The Elements of Political Science* (New York: Knopf, 1952), Chaps. 2, 9, 13-15, published in two vols., revised as *Politics and Government* (Colliers, 1962); and *The American Way of Government* (New York: Wiley, 1957), Chap. 8.

portionment. Amelioration can occur without further damage, if the stipulations of the preceding pages prevail. Furthermore, if the judiciary restrains its moves, it will permit a positive answer to the question "Can something more important be done to improve the representative structure of American State and local governments?"

Neither *Baker* v. *Carr,* nor the direct judicial and legislative consequences of that case thus far, is likely to help provide coordinated leadership in the nation, State, and locality; nor will it introduce a sense of community in the metropolises or better-operating smaller communities.[2] Men of quality and character are abundant in the United States but they are less and less to be discovered devoting their time to politics. Intellectually, they know they should be in public affairs. There are, for example, a number of programs operated by private associations such as corporations and unions to train leaders for political activity. An American foundation has encouraged in many colleges an intensified education in politics. Rarely have the programs succeeded in finding recruits for the active civic leadership of the nation.[3] People cannot, in the first place, perceive in what they are taught any continuously good and meaningful activity. Those who enter politics apprehend its triviality, the tangle of legalities and formalities, and the hopelessness of pleasing everyone. There is a number of causes for the scarcity of political leadership on all levels of politics in America. Only that connected with apportionment can be explained here. The chief fact of the existing apportionment is plain. Legislators literally do not know what they are representing. "The people," it is said, but that is no reply. It is a permissible evasion. It is like saying "I represent the good." Merely personal cliques are helped to come to a focus in the

---

[2] Cf. Wheeler and Bebout, "After Reapportionment," *op. cit.,* 246. "Apathetic public concern, atrophied political organizations, the generally low visibility of state politics and the lack of positive leadership stand out vividly in the majority of States." (249)

[3] Cf. Andrew Hacker and J. D. Averbach, "Businessmen in Politics," *Law and Contemporary Problems* (Spring 1962), 266; Marvin Schick and Albert Somit, "The Failure to Teach Political Activity," *American Behavioral Scientist,* January 1963, 5.

constituencies of equal-populations districts or of districts that are voided of integrity owing to the common compromises of community boundaries with that doctrine. In addition, very large pressure groups can operate effectively and without responsibility owing to the anonymous character of the districts.

The communities of America consist of all those clusters of human relations—needs, hopes, work, and sociability—that form in the course of social life. If these groups mean anything in themselves—and I believe they mean more than any other social fact except the dignity of the individual person—then they must have a value when projected into the larger forms of society—the county or metropolis, the State, the nation, and the world. Therefore, a system of apportionment must seek to promote these highly important human associations. If possible the villages, towns, and cities in themselves should be aided to express their ways of life in the higher councils. If they cannot all be accommodated directly, they should be served by counties that are themselves meaningful and, so far as the union is concerned, in States (or natural regions). The worst set of problems in American government today, after race relations, lies in metropolitan government. These giant aggregates are like vast protoplasms without spirit, muscle, and brain. They can be helped to organize and control themselves if appropriately represented. An apportionment that lends some shape to them as communities can assist their total development, and help provide them with leadership. For example, it is probable that the City of New York, with its suburban counties, if represented by only ten seats at large in the New York Assembly, would gain more of a political character and integrity, and achieve more total planning and legitimate State support than it gets now with several times that many seats or would get if it had additional seats in accord with the equal-populations principle.

It is not intended, however, that this kind of community representation should be the only kind provided the people. Groups other than geographical communities exist in abundance in our society. They are the voluntary associations and occupational groups. Teachers, communication workers, professional people, farmers, and a number of other groups live in communities of their own, none the less vital and important for not being geographical in nature. Unknown to the general public, who thinks of them only as lobbies, they are fairly well organized, active in political, economic and civic life and worthy of recognition by most criteria of what should be represented in representative government. Sooner or later they will be officially recognized. They already have a great many informal, extra-legal, and even legal obligations and responsibilities.

Alongside such groups stand more freely forming associations for ideas, sometimes manifested through leading personalities. Regional planning groups, leagues of voters, child welfare groups, and educational reform groups are illustrations. Free apportionment, which is provided for in proportional representation permits the alignment of idea and personality groups better than any other known system. The States need some elements of initiative, daring, and controversiality. Loose social groupings and new groups forming in the society also may be encouraged by the system of proportional representation.

Obviously, the solution to problems of such large scope cannot be a single one. Much less can it rest in the reform of apportionment. Yet apportionment and matters related closely to it can be used as an instrument of reform.

An apportionment system should be aimed at facilitating the tasks of government in a way that will preserve the basic principles of representative government. In the second chapter, these were named as *a pervasive doctrine of the consent of the people as the basis of government, provision for the entry of various kinds of opinions and interests into the political process and legislation, limits on the extent to which dissenting groups can be coerced,* and *a rule of law.*

Picture again the functions of legislators, as were related earlier. The legislator expresses sentiments of people and groups. He invents and plans law. He controls the executive and administration. He performs services to constituents. He does these all in concert with many others, so his fifth function is to cooperate. It may be

168

noted that there is a large measure of correspondence between the functions of the legislator and the basic principles of representative government. Figure 9 below outlines the connections between the principles and the functions. It also relates both to the method of apportionment that is appropriate to each. Finally it connects the method of apportionment to the major problems of State government today. Each principle of government can be served by a method of apportionment. Each function can be facilitated by some method of apportionment. Each major problem can be approached by a method of apportionment.

Apportionment in the Next Generation

The immediate reform of apportionment must consist of suggestions for coping with the subject in the legislature and dealing with it in the courts. The State legislatures can best resist destructive tides by carrying out their own State laws. Obviously, in some cases the degree of malapportionment has risen too high to be justifiably tolerated. They can also begin to assign to the many university governmental research bureaus more research on the techniques and effects of devices of government. If only one legislature in the country (or one university research bureau supported by a legislature) had set up a long-term fundamental research program of this sort, the whole setting today would be altered for the better. If the same citizen groups that are erroneously pressing the current attack on apportionment would join the State legislators in a more important and necessary attack on the problems of the future federalism and reframe their methods, they could help create a better representative democracy.[4] It is not too early to consider reforms that point in new directions in the field of apportionment. The figure already presented contains suggestions for new trends. With intensive study and gradual innovation, the country can be prepared for a system, which, once settled upon, might well endure for centuries.

---

[4] Wheeler and Bebout, *op. cit.*

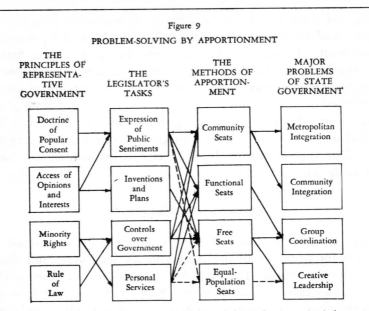

Figure 9

PROBLEM-SOLVING BY APPORTIONMENT

The arrows indicate the major ways in which basic principles connect with legislative operating tasks and these in turn with the methods of apportioning seats in the legislature and finally with the chief current problems. Equal-population seats are mentioned because they are so common, but are differentiated by dotted lines because they do little for metropolitan integration, community integration, group and idea coordination, or creative leadership. They do, however, encourage personal services without any larger intervening socially desirable frame. As the chart implies, State apportionments should move towards more community, functional, and free seats and away from equal-population districts created by territorial survey.

Within 50 years, variations of the new system may be possible and desirable in a number of States. In that time constitutional representation and apportionment might approach a basic form that can be foreseen here. This model is offered solely for orientation and discussion. In politics, as in medicine, prescription should follow only after examination of the individual case.

There would be three basic systems of apportionment in the major assembly of this hypothetical State, one based on *communities,* a second based on *functional* alignments, and a third based on *free populations.* (The basis for each is not intended to preclude the workings of the other basis informally within it.) [5]

The major assembly of the State would consist of "X" members, of three classes. Each eligible voter would cast a vote on whichever one he pleased of three lists offered him: *community, functional,* or *free.*

Class 1. The first class would consist of community members, totalling 40 percent of all seats. The districts of each of the members would be the following: one for each governmental or combined governmental region of not less than 1/40 X of the population of the State. (Everyone would fall into one of these territorial groupings.)

Class 2. The second class would consist of members numbering 20 percent of the major assembly, chosen as follows: one member for each of the top .20 X occupational categories of the State, said categories to correspond to a list of major categories of employment in the State, including housewives and high school and college students as categories, and reserving the 20th category for all those not otherwise grouped. A panel of seven persons could be formed, appointed three by the legislature, two by the Governor and two by the Supreme Court. The panel would define the categories and the suffrage requirement within them.

Class 3. The third class would consist of *free members* amounting to 40 percent of the legislature. These would be apportioned by population to counties, groups of counties, and metropolitan districts. They would be elected by plurality (majority) election in counties with one or two members and by the Hare system of proportional representation elsewhere. (This system permits persons anywhere within the large district to combine into constituencies in the process of voting for candidates, who are elected in the present case when they receive roughly 1/.40 X of the ballots cast. The effect would be to give any sizable group of persons with a program or an ideology a voice in the legislature. [6]

---

[5] Cf. Chapter 2, pp. 11-19.

[6] An example: If the major assembly had 100 members, 40 would be *community* members, 20 *functional* members, and 40 *free* members.

Elections would be triennial and separate from presidential elections. Reapportionment would be simple and accomplished every 20 years. If, after the first apportionment, the second does not occur between the 19th and the 20th years, the governor would appoint a commission composed of one community, one functional, and one free-quota assemblyman to present a plan within several months. The plan would go into effect in the next subsequent election: if the commissioners failed to present such a plan, they would have committed a misdemeanor.

A second chamber, to my way of thinking, appears desirable if it is small and placed in close connection with the governor of the State. It would be useful in giving the governor honest advice and acting as watchdog over the administration of the State. Its members should number under a score. They should be elected from no more than three regions of the State by limited vote that would permit no party to win all the offices in any region.

It must be emphasized that the proportions of the three classes would vary from State to State, as would other parts of the representative system.

Caution and care should be exercised in the prescription of any system of apportionment. The human and governmental costs of reapportionments are high; they should only be undertaken with some strong purpose in mind. Nevada is not New York, nor Alaska Florida. In any case, the reform of apportionment has to be approached in the full light of the many other features of representative government.[7] The figure just presented is indicative only. It may

---

[7] Other reforms are needed if State legislatures are to be restored to a full effective role. Raising the status of legislators by better working conditions and more staff services will improve the quality of legislators and the relations of representatives and constituents. A full reporting of debates would focus more informed attention on legislative proceedings. Additional work responsibilities should be placed upon legislators in connection with State government to enhance their knowledge and skills, and to permit their pay to reach a full-time base. Placing legislators in important ex-officio positions throughout the State, such as on educational boards, regulatory commissions and metropolitan boards, will lift their status.

be of help to those who seek the broadest base for an elective system and seek to be guided by evidence and logic. But caution need not mean inaction or trivial and meaningless action.

These long-range suggestions are offered with an appropriate sense of realism. Proportional representation has walked a rocky path in America, and it is still recommended here. To put it into practice would require much leadership and popular education. While I cannot do more than suggest it here, those who are concerned with apportionment might do well to examine its advantages and disadvantages as a part of a larger system of representation. Other ideas advanced here may also find acceptance difficult to achieve. Despite the heavy role played by voluntary associations in the legislative process and the numerous beginnings of a formalization of that role, many persons are reluctant to make their responsibility commensurate with their power.

We cannot know what form any government will take in the next generation, and the surest guess of all is to be pessimistic and state that the future will be what exists today, as modified by disaster. If, rather than guessing, we wish to attempt some control, then we should perhaps be more active in creating the instruments of control

---

Undertaking more ambitious State projects in collaboration with non-governmental groups in education, in recreation and conservation, industrial planning, agriculture, and crime control would also help orient the State legislator to a new set of roles. The State legislator's job is still regarded in in the large as was that of the Member of the Commons in the 18th century when you could buy a vote for a roast beef dinner, a pint of ale, and a guinea. Change of assembly and house names, if needs be, might be wise: a man acts as he is called. The names could be more functional in the language of 20th century administrative leadership. A "State Civic Management Council" would *ipso nomine* introduce some progressive change in legislative work. District offices of legislators should be financed by the State treasury and steps should be taken to organize better and more broadly the social and informative functions of legislators with respect to their constituents. In regard to the constituency, serious consideration should be given to changing suffrage requirements to permit citizens to vote where they work as an alternative to voting where they live. This would, of course, cause trouble to the notion of equal-populations in apportionment, but the fallacies of that notion have already been exposed.

than we have been. It is painfully obvious that very little is known about the real effects of different ways of managing government. State governments, universities, and foundations have been unaware of the need for research in State government. They have been satisfied with trivial, superficial, and mediocre work. In a society that has learned how research and development budgets running to 10 percent of gross expenditures can pave the way to booming industries and science, it is no longer anti-climactic to end even a book on apportionment with a recommendation for more knowledge of a more profound kind. The present struggle over apportionment, like so many others in history, began in ignorance and continued in ignorance. Unless saner minds and broader visions take control, it will end as a triumph of ignorance.

EPILOGUE

IN THE LARGE THEATRE of activity on apportionment, stretching from Florida to Hawaii, several major forces of the past and future are at work. The rule of law is being tested in the familiar American manner; it begins as a split in the highest Court of the land. There is a scattering of shot into the darkness and the debate is taken up everywhere. The courts, it seems, are killing that which they love best—the constitutional order.

The fatal means is an excess of constitutional authority, inflicted upon the original and fundamental institution of the United States —federalism, the most successful federalism the world has known.

The accomplice is the egalitarian doctrine, patron goddess of majoritarians and of a retinue of interests more enthusiastic than devout. The egalitarian doctrine is expressed in one of its many traditional forms, as a demand for equal-populations districts. By clamor and in haste, that which is a doctrine is enshrined as part of the law of the land to be enforced by the courts.

It matters little that the egalitarian doctrine is impossible to specify in the practices of apportionment; it is effectively a symbol around which can rally a variety of interests, who in the eternal way of disciples are half aware and half blind. So what has never been the law of the land is to be made such. Federalism and the rule of law are being placed clearly and presently in danger of damage as a result of many extraordinary measures that courts and legislatures are taking or may be forced to take to admit the egalitarian dogma.

THE EQUAL-POPULATIONS doctrine would bring worse conditions, if applied, than result from the systems of apportionment in being. Even if the grave constitutional issues of judicial power and federalism were absent, and even if a more rational policymaking mechanism than the courts was used to make the changes, this would be so. For the evil is in the nature of the dogma. Moreover, the equal-populations apportionment brings about a defective organization of public opinion and policy activity.

AT THE SAME TIME, the existing system is in need of reform. Even if malapportionment were reduced, as it should be, the existing system in the United States has serious defects:

In many jurisdictions, the present systems of apportionment are neither community-oriented nor population-oriented, but fall in between. Consequently, satisfactory representation is being provided for too few people and interests.

The existing apportionment systems do not recognize the need for metropolitan government. Consequently, they do not contribute to solving one of the worst problems of American domestic politics—the chaotic and miserable government of the large cities.

The existing apportionment systems contribute very little to attracting leadership to politics. They encourage civic apathy among ordinary citizens as well.

PROVIDED THAT the courts do not force the apportionment systems of the country into a rigid egalitarian mold, the government of the States, localities, and nation can and should explore new methods of representation. In general, these should seek to promote the State legislatures to a higher level of mission and performance. They should try to provide greater connections between the natural communities of the State and the State government. They should begin to formalize and make responsible the many natural channels of functional government dug by the representation of living interests. To make votes count best, they cannot be made equal.

If the States proceed along these lines, with the understanding and at the prodding of experts on the metropolis, informed citizens, and federal officials, a new and stronger federalism will result. If nothing like this occurs, we shall witness our country moving toward a mechanical view of citizenship and representation with an irrevocable consequent regimentation of government and a further decline of civic initiative throughout the nation.

INDEX